What People Are Saying About
The Home Office From Hell Cure

"Jeff Landers treats a serious subject with humor, style and wisdom. If you have a home office, his cure is just what the home office doctor ordered."
—Jay Conrad Levinson, "The Father of Guerrilla Marketing"

"Jeff has put together a nuts-and-bolts guide to getting unstuck from your dreary home office existence. Now it's up to you to get going."
—Seth Godin, Co-author of Guerrilla Marketing for the Home-Based Business

"Mr. Landers isn't my favorite stand-up-comic, but he can keep you laughing while you get out of your home office from hell! Great read."
— Michael E. Gerber, Author of The E-Myth books

"Jeff Landers says it like it is! A quick, fun, no-nonsense read that will make a big difference in starting and growing your homebased business!"
—Barbara Corcoran, founder of The Corcoran Group, a real estate company she began from her living room with a $1000 loan and later sold for $66 million.

"Easy to read, fun to page through, and packed with great advice for homebased entrepreneurs that want to make their business visions a reality. Jeff Landers can help you have a much better business."
—W. Kenneth Yancey, Jr., CEO of SCORE – Counselors to America's Small Business

The Home Office From Hell Cure

Transform Your Underperforming Time-Sucking Homebased Business into a Runaway Success

Jeffrey A. Landers

Entrepreneur.
Press

Jeff Landers has been involved in commercial real estate for more than three decades. He is a serial entrepreneur who has founded five businesses and has been advising small businesses since 1988. His company, Home Office Success, Inc., has helped thousands of homebased businesses become more professional, more productive, and more profitable.

Publisher: Jere L. Calmes
Cover Design: Desktop Miracles
Production and Composition: CWL Publishing Enterprises, Inc., Madison, Wisconsin, www.cwlpub.com

ISBN-13: 978-1-59918-167-7

Library of Congress Cataloging-in-Publication Data

Landers, Jeffrey A.
  The home office from hell cure / by Jeffrey A. Landers.
    p. cm.
  ISBN-13: 978-1-59918-167-7 (alk. paper)
  1. Home-based businesses—Management. 2. Home-based businesses—Marketing. 3. Entrepreneurship. 4. Success in business. I. Title.
  HD62.38.L36 2008
  658'.0412—dc22

                                                                      2008004595

Printed in Canada

Author's Copyright Notice

Support Entrepreneurship

Fifty percent of all author royalties from this book are
donated to Non-Profits that support Entrepreneurship, including:

SCORE (score.org)

National Association of Women Business Owners (nawbo.org)

Association of Small Business Development Centers (asbdc-us.org)

Dedication

To my amazing and wonderful wife, Barbara
Any success I have, I owe to you.
None of this would have been possible without your love,
encouragement and wicked sense of humor.

To my fantastic daughters, Alyse and Joanna
Having you makes me the richest man in the world.

I would also like to give special thanks to my mother, Edith,
who taught me that anything is possible and who made many sacrifices
in her life to make mine better. And to my mother-in-law, June,
who is probably my biggest cheerleader.

I love you all.

Contents

Foreword

By George H. Ross
Executive Vice President and Senior Counsel, The Trump Organization
Co-star of the TV show The Apprentice

I worked with Donald Trump on his first big deal, turning the unglamorous Commodore Hotel into the spectacular Grand Hyatt. This was a complex deal with a lot of drama. There were feuding parties, disputes, arbitrations, lawsuits, compromises, delays, publicity and, ultimately, triumph. I admit there were plenty of times I didn't think that deal was going to come together.

To be truthful, I thought it was a dream that might never become a reality.

But it was Donald's dream and he was persistent. I watched Donald will the Grand Hyatt into existence. And what he did is a lesson to all of us in business. Whether you are running a Fortune 500 company or cobbling together a business in your basement, you must focus on your vision. You must be forceful and unrelenting even when people around you think your dream is impossible or foolish. You must take your lumps and keep moving forward.

Most of all, you should enjoy the ride. You should be excited to get out of bed and get to work. You can't have a great company if you aren't inspired by what it can be. If you're not, no one else will be either.

You're probably reading this because you aren't feeling great about your business. Maybe the dream you had for your homebased business has run into a roadblock. It happens. If you are sitting in your very own Home Office From Hell you're probably feeling extremely uninspired right now. I bet your bank account is, too. I bet your feeling of failure overshadows your whole life.

So, if that's you, you're on the road to recovery by reading Jeff's book. That means you're already planning to change the operation and outlook of your business and that's the first step. What's the next step? Start reading. Jeff has set this book up so that you can actually sit down and *do* something every day to change your business. And since success begets success, take it from me that if you work on improving your business a little bit every day, you'll have a much better business 100 days from now.

You can read *The Home Office From Hell Cure,* enjoy it, learn a few things, and then put it down and go back to dreaming about the business you wish were yours. Or you can read it, implement a few key ideas and start working on improving your business *today*. You can talk a good game or you can do what's necessary to make it happen. The choice is yours.

I've often said that when building the Grand Hyatt, Donald was a bit like Babe Ruth, pointing to center field and willing that home run to happen. Now, you're at bat. Find your inner Babe, point to the grandstand and let ' er rip!

Introduction

There is no businessperson gutsier than the homebased entrepreneur.

Yes, it's a big statement to make and some may disagree, but I believe it down to my bones. You, the homebased businessowner, are a maverick.

You take a kernel of an idea and turn it into something real and valuable. First, you give up the security of the corporate world—its 401(k)s, steady paychecks, and mandatory vacation time. Then you max out your credit cards and home equity. You brave the naysayers and the doubters (sometimes in your own families). You nod your head politely, undeterred in the pursuit of your dream.

You are not content to go to work for some corporate monolith or, even worse, to help someone else fulfill his dreams. You know there is something better out there— something you can call your own. More importantly, you know you are good enough to make it happen. So, you do it. In my book that makes you a maverick.

Along the way, you've probably signed up for the best seminars and boot camps, read the latest business books, and spent thousands of dollars every year trying to get your business out of a rut and onto the next level. That's what smart businesspeople do, right? They invest in themselves. They do their homework.

Right. But what if all that is useless to the success of your business?

An amazing thought, but not only do I believe that most of it is useless, it actually might be counterproductive! I talk to entrepreneurs every day and I believe many of you fall into the trap of spending way too much time daydreaming and not enough time doing. Some of you—and you know who you are—would rather buy the latest business book than actually do something concrete to move your business forward.

It may feel like you're doing something, but you're really not. This is just the beginning of what is strangling your small business and pummeling your dreams of success.

Mark my words—*doing* is the key. There is no shortage of business theory and philosophy out there, but the key is getting up and doing something. It is all about taking that first step, then the next, and the next. Reading a business book may give you some great ideas to change your business, but actually putting one foot in front of the other is going to make it happen.

That's where *The Home Office From Hell Cure* can help. I've put together step-by-step, manageable, daily tasks to get you onto a schedule that will take your business to a whole new level in only 100 days.

No more day-long seminars that load you up with inspirational but impractical theory, and keep you away from your business for a day or more. No more pouring over theory that looks great on paper, only to wonder how to apply it to your real-life business.

My book breaks down the actual tasks you must do every day, and gives you a checklist so you can get it done. No secret formulas or mysterious business wisdoms that only a handful of super-gurus in the world know about. Just the simple, one-step-at-a-time, everyday tasks you need to do to pull your business out of the doldrums.

The Home Office From Hell Cure is designed to help two types of homebased entrepreneurs. I'm sure you fit into one of these categories: (1) Growth Mavens, who want to build their own small empire and need to move into a "real" office space and start hiring staff, and (2) Lifestyle Gurus, who want to remain at home and work in their pajamas while still making a comfortable six-figure income.

For the Growth Mavens reading this, *The Home Office From Hell Cure* shows you how to get out of your home office and into a "real" office by using office space that can be rented afford-ably and without long-term commitment. It tells you how and why you need to hire low-cost staff to handle time-consuming, non-income-producing, administrative tasks, so you can focus on high-revenue-generating items.

For Lifestyle Gurus, the book tells you how to use virtual office space to make your business appear larger and more professional, while giving you the steps to outsource jobs that take you away from the work that is really crucial to your business.

My book teaches both types of entrepreneurs how to use simple, tried-and-true, PR and pub-licity vehicles to become a "Nexpert," or niche expert, in your field, and how to parlay that public image and visibility into new revenue streams for your business.

Each goal is broken down into small, super-manageable tasks that you can do every day to get your business moving and out of its rut. No philosophy lessons. Just good ol' practical advice broken down into baby steps that set you up to succeed.

Save your money and throw away the registration form for that next boot camp and read just one more business book—one that will keep you moving every day toward a more successful business and a better life.

Really, you have the power to change your business in only 100 days. By the time you finish reading this book and working through the daily activities, you will have a business that is more professional, more productive, and more profitable than the one you started with.

Isn't it time to transform your unproductive, time-sucking homebased business into a runaway success?

Be a maverick. Carpe diem!

How to Use This Book

How is this book organized?

The purpose of this book is to provide a "cure" for those homebased businesses that suffer from the business-killing disease of stagnation.

If you're a homebased entrepreneur and you feel that, in spite of all your efforts, you're still treading water and you can't seem to move your business forward no matter what (or maybe even worse—you're starting to fall behind), then reading this book and doing the simple daily tasks will get your business back on track and moving ahead (way ahead) in only 100 days.

Think of this book as the defibrillator you need to jump-start your homebased business back to life. Then and only then will you be able to start building and growing the business you've always wanted.

The first thing you do in this book is decide if you really have a Home Office From Hell in the first place. I'm not talking about a messy desk or unorganized files here—I'm talking about your business that is not even close to operating on all six cylinders. I put it right out there for you, so if you have any doubt whether yours is a Home Office From Hell, we answer it immediately.

Then, we find out exactly what kind of homebased entrepreneur you are (bet you didn't know that there was more than one). Are you a Growth Maven, who wants to build your own mini-empire, or are you a Lifestyle Guru, who wants to stay small and at home while being able to bring in a comfortable six-figure income? This is a critical distinction and helps us know how best to grow your business.

You answer this question by taking a quick quiz designed to get you thinking about your goals for you and your business. Once you know that, we're off to the races.

Growth Mavens will learn:

- Why you must get out of your home office and into a "real" office.
- How to make the move cheaply and without much disruption.
- How to affordably and easily hire staff to get the time-sucking jobs off your plate so you can focus your full attention on the revenue-generating work and not the administrative stuff.

Lifestyle Gurus will learn:

- Why you must have a virtual office space to make your business look bigger and be more competitive, and why that's important.
- How to affordably outsource grunt work to virtual assistants so you can focus your full attention on the revenue-generating work and not the administrative stuff.

Then comes the fun part. I help you become an expert in your field in less than 100 days!

That's right, I give you the step-by-step plan that will help you become what I call a "Nexpert," a niche expert.

Here's what you will do as a Nexpert to grow your business:

- Write one 500-word article (as an expert in your field) and get it published.
- Write a speech and set up two speaking engagements in front of a roomful of potential clients.
- Write a Tips Booklet that you'll use as a free giveaway when you are networking.
- Write and send out a press release and set up two interviews with the press.
- Prepare and record one tele-seminar for potential customers and important clients.

Whew! That sounds like a lot of work…and it is. But you are only going to do a little every day.

It won't be overwhelming. I'll give you daily assignments that will move you closer each day, one small step at a time, to a better, more visible, more financially sound business.

What do I have to do?

Your role is critical here. You can't simply read this book, put it on your bookshelf, and hope your business improves through osmosis. It won't. You will have to work the steps.

In each section, I give you easy, daily tasks that make growing and running your business more manageable. (For reference, I've laid out the complete 100 Day Plan for you, day by day, in the Appendix.) Your job is to commit some time each day to working the tasks. The idea is that you do a little each day and keep moving yourself forward.

After only 100 days, you'll see big changes in your business.

Do I have to read everything in this book to make it work for me?

No. If you have zero interest in building a mini-empire, love working from home, but just want to make more money, have better clients, and enjoy more leisure time, then feel free to skip the parts designed for the Growth Maven entrepreneurs who are chomping at the bit to move into a "real" office, start hiring employees, and become the next Jeff Bezos.

You have my permission to just read the stuff that works for you. On the other hand, if you want to sneak in and see what the other half is doing, you have my blessing.

Do I have to do every task in this book to make it work for me?

Good question. I want to emphasize here that you should try to do each of the steps as they are set out. Why? Because I don't want you to get off track.

The minute you stop doing daily assignments, there is the temptation to stop altogether and stay in your home office rut—so I strongly suggest you do the tasks every day. Make it a habit. It should be in permanent ink on your calendar.

There are exceptions, however, and I wouldn't want to be completely inflexible. So for instance, maybe public speaking is too terrifying for you or not the best way to reach your potential customers; however, you are a crack writer and putting out great Nexpert columns is more suited to your strengths and will get you more attention. If so, I encourage you to play to your strengths.

Cut the speech and write more articles if that works for you. The idea is to get something cooking, talk to your potential customers, get the word out about who you are and what you're doing. Make each task a catalyst for action, so that you will have a more professional, more productive, and more profitable business in only 100 days.

Okay, Jeff ... Where do I start?
Start with Chapter 1.

I made the chapters brief for a reason. See if you really have a Home Office From Hell. See if today is really the day you are going to make a change.

If so, then move to the next section, "What Kind of Entrepreneur Am I?" Think about what you want to achieve. Then, take the quiz in Chapter 10. Once you know the answer to that question, there is no stopping you. Just follow the steps as they're described and do one small task for your business every day.

It's that simple—one small task every day to a better business.

It can happen, if you carpe diem.

Acknowledgments

Writing a book is a huge endeavor, especially for a first-time author.

There is no way that this book would ever have seen the light of day without the help and support of many people.

Therefore, I would like to offer my thanks and gratitude to the following people:

Jere Calmes, Editorial Director, Entrepreneur Press—Who immediately "got it" upon reading my manuscript and has been my steadfast champion ever since.

Ken Yancey, CEO of SCORE—Who introduced me to Jere. If not for Ken, this book would probably have remained in my head. Ken has been a great friend to me and every entrepreneur should become best friends with SCORE.

Kim Foster, a good friend—who helped turn my ideas, expertise and feeble attempts at writing into a fantastic and saleable manuscript. Her advice, encouragement, humor and writing skills were vital to this project. Nothing would have happened without her.

John Woods and his group at CWL Publishing Enterprises, Sarah White, Dale Dean, and Marg Sumner, were responsible for taking the manuscript and turning it into the book you now hold.

Laura Anderton—Her cartoons gave life to my written words.

Leanne Harvey, Director of Marketing, Entrepreneur Press—Her marketing skills helped get this book into your hands.

George H. Ross, EVP, The Trump Organization, and co-star of the TV show, *The Apprentice*—George and I have only met twice, yet he is one of the nicest and most generous people I know. The fact that he took the time out of his unbelievably busy schedule to read my manuscript and write the Foreword for this book speaks volumes about the person that is known as Donald Trump's right-hand man. I am truly grateful to George.

Barbara Corcoran, Jay Conrad Levinson, Michael E. Gerber, and Seth Godin—None of whom knew me from a hole in the wall, yet were kind enough to read my manuscript and provide me with some great blurbs for this book. I very much appreciate their generosity.

Lloyd Jassin, Esq., my attorney—Who did a fabulous job of negotiating my contract with Entrepreneur and got me as much as he could without blowing the deal.

I'd also like to thank the many homebased entrepreneurs who entered The Home Office From Hell® contests and their many entries, both humorous and poignant, that were the genesis for this book.

And special thanks to my wife, Barbara, and my daughters, Alyse and Joanna, who make every day a wonderful day.

Part

Is My Home Office Really
The Home Office From Hell?

" If you're going through hell, keep going..."

—*Winston Churchill*

Chapter 1. What Exactly Is a Home Office From Hell?

If you've picked up this book, you probably think you have a little problem with your home office and, maybe, your business in general. At the very least, you suspect there might be room for improvement. Excellent! Because you can't have the business of your dreams unless you first admit that what you're doing isn't working perfectly.

So what exactly is a Home Office From Hell, and how do you know if you need the Cure? Well, here's my definition of a business-killing home office. See if any of this rings a bell.

Home Office From Hell \ hohm-aw-fis-frum-hel \ Noun:

1. Pertaining to or being about a completely dysfunctional, client-repelling office space in the home that makes one lose money. Also, the scene of many business-killing behaviors, including but not limited to: the Saint Bernard scaring away the FedEx guy, clients sitting in folding chairs in the hallway for meetings, toddlers answering the business phone and introducing themselves to new clients, and/or colleagues picturing you in your underwear while you are on a teleconference call.
2. An office that more resembles a playroom than a professional space. The space might include: piles of papers on the TV, last night's burrito stuck to the client proposal, clothes pins and masking tape holding together the fax machine, and/or dirty diapers in the file cabinet.

Example of the phrase used in a sentence:

The entrepreneur's business tanked because his clients took one look at his *Home Office From Hell* and assumed that his work would be just as disorganized and unprofessional.

Chapter 2. Do You Have a Home Office From Hell? Yes, I'm Talking to You.

If you operate a homebased business, you are probably ready to say something like, "Now, hold on there, buddy…my home office isn't so bad. Sure it's not ideal and there was that mishap with my newborn screaming bloody murder while I was on the phone with Tokyo, but my clients know I'm a professional."

To that I say, "Oh, really?"

Make no mistake—your clients only know what they see and hear from you. If they see that you have no place to meet them but Starbucks, they won't take you seriously. If you can't get packages delivered to your house because your dog nearly killed the UPS guy, they won't think you are serious about your business. If your mother-in-law interrupted your last meeting to remind you to pick up green beans at the supermarket, you will not be able to stand up to the competition.

Why? Because your competitors, whoever they are, are serious. They want your clients. They look polished. They have great presentations. A cool boardroom. Impressive offices and support staff. They have smooth pitches and people have heard their names before. They look big, even if they aren't. They have put full value on growing their businesses.

You, on the other hand, have a makeshift desk in the third bedroom. You have peanut-butter-and-jelly stains on your keyboard. You have an office that is the "best-kept secret" in the business. You have a business that's stuck in neutral.

Want to get moving? Keep reading.

Chapter 3. The Ten Signs You've Got a Home Office From Hell

Still in denial? Okay, check out this list. If any of this sounds even vaguely familiar, you may have a Home Office From Hell. (And by the way, all ten of these stories came from real entrepreneurs who wrote to me during our annual Home Office From Hell Contest—so no worries, you aren't alone.)

Sign number 10: "I want to hire an assistant, but we'd have to share a chair."

If your business is expanding faster than you have office furniture for, or you are meeting with your clients in the hallway, then you have a Home Office From Hell.

Sign number 9: "My husband thinks I need to get a real job."

If your husband or wife thinks that you spend your entire day chatting with the neighbors, or your mother-in-law is convinced you are running a drug cartel out of your living room, then you have a Home Office From Hell.

Sign number 8: "My friends think that working at home means I never miss *Days of Our Lives.*"

If you are like Rodney Dangerfield and you "don't get no respect" because your friends think you catch every episode of Dr. Phil and sleep until noon, then you have a Home Office From Hell.

Sign number 7: "Starbucks is starting to encroach on my profits."

If you are conducting all your big meetings in the Science Fiction section of Barnes and Noble or you are working on your sixth Grande Frappuccino, then you have a Home Office From Hell.

Sign number 6: "I realized today at 4 p.m. that I was still wearing pajamas."

If your idea of networking is talking to the cat, and you haven't been in a shower or out of the house in over a week, then you have a Home Office From Hell.

Sign number 5: "I could die here and no one would ever know."

If you worry that it might be the smell that finally gets people to inquire about your business, then you have a Home Office From Hell.

Sign number 4: "Why did God invent Oprah? How are we supposed to work when Oprah is on?"

If you are overwhelmed by the urge to climb back into bed or regularly feel a deep longing to do several loads of laundry in the middle of the business day, then you have a Home Office From Hell.

Sign number 3: "No, the baby doesn't go in the playpen. Important papers go in there so the baby can't get at them."

If you find yourself picking Cheerios out of your laptop, chasing the kids around the kitchen while conference-calling Stuttgart, and wiping peanut butter off your client's work, then you have a Home Office From Hell.

Sign number 2: I feel like I live at the office…wait! I do!

If your workday ends two minutes before you drop into bed, or you are taking 4 A.M. phone calls from sleepless clients, then you have a Home Office From Hell.

And last but not least…

Sign number 1: "Since you're home all day anyway, I need a favor…"

If you are picking up your wife's laundry, driving your friend to the airport, or running errands for your neighbors in the middle of your workday, then you have a Home Office From Hell.

Chapter 4. Sitting in Your Underwear at Your Computer Doesn't Make You an Entrepreneur.

Don't be fooled. Just because you have a desk and a stapler, that doesn't make you an entrepreneur. Entrepreneurs do not define themselves as they are today. They define themselves by who they will be tomorrow. They are visionaries. They are comfortable assuming a lot of risk today to build their business for tomorrow.

They are not fearless, but they eat the fear and move forward anyway. They conquer their fear by doing something—one small step at a time. They put one foot in front of the other until they have walked themselves out of the ditch. They are always moving toward the future. They are not stuck in one place. Entrepreneurs are active.

If you are rolling out of bed and sitting at your desk in your basement, trudging through the same old routines, doing the same old things that are not moving your business forward, if you are flicking pencils at the ceiling and wondering why the dream of *having* your own business is better than actually having your own business, then you are not being entrepreneurial.

Today is the time for you to do something different. It is time for you to summon your inner maverick. It is time for you to become the visionary for your own business—to take one small, tiny step toward the company you dreamed of having when you were sitting in that cubicle working for your overbearing bosses and that soulless corporation.

It is time to go from ordinary to extraordinary. Today is the day to become an entrepreneur.

A Regular Guy Makes It Big

A regular guy works at a Wall Street firm studying market trends. He sees a trend that no one else has spotted. He has daydreamed about starting his own business. He decides to take the leap. He packs up his stuff and quits his job.

He sets up a home office in his two-bedroom house. Free at last! No more listening to his inept boss. The regular guy is now calling the shots. He brings his wife into the business and hits his folks up for a sizable investment. The future is bright.

He runs extension cords out to the garage to operate his computers and uses doors from Home Depot as desks. Life is pretty chaotic, but it soon pays off.

A month later, this guy is selling product in all 50 states and 45 countries. Two months later, he's bringing in $20,000 a week in revenue.

Sounds implausible, right? Well, this regular guy is named Jeff Bezos and his multi-billion-dollar company, Amazon.com, proves that you can start a business in your home and use it as a launch pad for success.

Ask yourself, "Why did I start my homebased business?"

Didn't you start out trying to create something amazing?

You can still do it. It's not too late. Remember, Jeff Bezos was just a regular guy—albeit a very smart and hard-working regular guy—working at his computer on top of an unfinished door. And he turned that meager beginning into something extraordinary.

If a regular guy can create something extraordinary, why not you, too?

Part 2

What Kind of Entrepreneur Am I?

"Hope is not a strategy"

—General George Custer

Chapter 5. Should I Build an Empire? Or Keep It Small?

Before you can begin to cure your ailing business and become a thriving entrepreneur, you must know who you really are and what you really want.

Years ago, a writer friend of mine named Julia took a job as a speechwriter with one of the big accounting firms. She took the job because it paid very well and came with a great deal of status (she would be writing speeches for the CEO). She was young and most of her friends held low-paying administrative jobs. They all urged Julia to take the job and saw this as the springboard that would launch her career.

So Julia took the plunge. She accepted the big paycheck and the beeper and walked into her windowed office at 8 A.M. and left sometime after 9 P.M. every night.

At first, when the beeper interrupted her dates and time with friends, she felt important. She was so badly needed. These guys couldn't live without her. She must be important. Her friends and family admired her and she loved the attention.

But this wore off quickly.

When we spoke, she told me that the job was not what she had imagined. She lamented that she had stopped writing her novel, and rarely had time to do anything with friends and family. She felt smothered by her boss, the CEO. She secretly admired her friends who were working their way up through the ranks and doing things they loved. She couldn't imagine how she would tell her mother she hated her job—her mother was so proud of her. She asked my advice about what to do next.

I asked her some questions—about where she saw herself in ten years. How she wanted to fill each day. What did the perfect writing day look like for her?

What we found was that speech-writing was a perfectly reasonable job. Her employers had perfectly reasonable expectations. There was nothing wrong with the CEO. In fact, Julia admitted, many writers would be downright thrilled to be paid so well and to work with such interesting people.

The problem was that Julia was not the right fit for this job. When we talked about what she really wanted, none of it took place in a fancy high-rise, with a windowed office and set hours. She longed to write more magazine articles and finish her book. She wanted to manage her own hours and write about those projects that interested her.

She had no interest in building a large business. She wanted to stay small and do what she loved.

The status and the big paycheck were not nearly as important to her as they were to the people around her. It took her some time to realize that this job was *their* dream, not hers.

So, what's the moral of this tale? You can't make yourself happy—you can't have the business of your dreams—until you know who you really are and what you really want. Your business has to match you.

The first thing you have to decide is whether you want to stay small or build an empire.

Chapter 6. Are You a 'Growth Maven'?

'Growth Mavens' are fiercely ambitious. They do not think small.

The Growth Maven starts her business in her home office to keep expenses low, but is chomping at the bit to raise the company to new heights. Her dream is to grow from a single person company to a multi-employee company and maybe even larger. She thinks someday she will be like the mega-stars who originally started their companies as homebased businesses: Bill Gates, Martha Stewart, Jeff Bezos, Steve Jobs, and Michael Dell.

She isn't looking to settle down in her second-bedroom office and stay for any length of time. She is a visionary and she has one eye on the future. She knows she has to take plenty of risks—there will be times when her cash flow is crunched because she is expanding more rapidly than the profits are coming in—but she knows that the uncomfortable cycle of growth will be worth it when her company is gaining attention and picking up customers.

She knows there is no limit to the amount of money she can make, and she is dedicated to constantly innovating her products and services. But she has to get out of her house first. She has to take the first step.

Does this sound familiar? If you are a Growth Maven, you have to take the first steps to building your empire—you'll need to move to your first "real" office and bring on some staff. But you want to manage it so that the big leap doesn't drain your time, money, and resources. You want to set yourself up for growth and long-term success. You want customers to know your name and what you stand for. You want to develop a reputation and have a consistent stream of dialogue running between you and your customers.

It isn't easy, but if you are a Growth Maven, you can make it happen. This is your time to harness your inner maverick and make your vision a reality. Say good-bye to your Home Office From Hell, Growth Mavens. You're off to build an empire!

Chapter 7. Or a 'Lifestyle Guru'?

The 'Lifestyle Guru' made the dream happen the first day that he didn't go into the office.

His dream was to leave the soulless corporation behind and be his own boss. He hates the commute, the suit and tie, the cubicle, the office politics, and the crazy, overbearing bosses. He wants more—to not just feel like he is pushing paper until 6 o'clock. He wants to feel a sense of contribution and pride in his work. And he wants to do it his way.

He is psyched to be his own boss, have a flexible schedule, and decide for himself when to work and when to take time off. He wants to wear pajamas to work and knock off at 3 P.M. for a few hours so he can catch his kid's soccer match. He doesn't mind clearing out his e-mail in-box after his wife and kids are in bed. Sometimes he works on the weekends, sometimes he doesn't.

He knows there is a limit to the amount of money he can make, but he is bringing in a comfortable six-figure income and he has more leisure time to spend with his family and friends. When it works, it all feels pretty good.

If you are aspiring to be a Lifestyle Guru, you'll want to do a few things—increase your productivity, stay competitive, get better clients, and continue to make more money—all without compromising your lifestyle choices. Whew! Sounds like a tall order, right?

No way. The Lifestyle Gurus who are doing it successfully have a plan for making it work. They make themselves look big even when they're small. They outsource the things that both drain their time and aren't revenue-producing. And they get their customers' attention.

They aren't wasting away in their basement offices, hoping they'll get that next assignment. They are *out there*. They have a reputation for being professional, organized, and on the ball. They are constantly sending that message in everything they do.

It isn't a cakewalk, but if you are an aspiring Lifestyle Guru, you can make it happen. This is your time to harness your inner maverick and make your vision a reality.

So Lifestyle Gurus, get ready to eliminate the "From Hell" from your Home Office. You have a life to start living!

Chapter 8. The Secret of Momentum

I'm going to get a little philosophical on you and briefly talk about Jean Paul Sartre, the famous French playwright and philosopher.

Sartre believed that people often experience angst when they are deluged with too many choices. He believed the more choices we have in front of us, the more paralyzed we become by our own anxiety.

Which way should I go? How about this way? No! That might be a mistake! Maybe this way is better…what if I make the wrong decision?

And modern research bears this out—we human beings do better with a few specific black and white choices. But building a business is almost never about one or two clear-cut options. Entrepreneurs are faced with many nuance-laced options on a daily basis, and for some strange reason they always seem to be of the "do or die" variety.

As one of my clients told me, "When I worked for a big firm and made a mistake, the effects were barely felt by anyone. But now, with my small business, it doesn't take much for a small error in judgment to shake the company to the core."

He continued, "Just thinking about it makes me want to take the day off."

Ah, angst! Sartre, the old boy, was right on the money. When faced with too many choices, a confused mind will do *absolutely nothing!*

So we just sit there, staring at our blank desk calendars, hoping our phones will ring, or a new client will somehow fall into our laps. And we stick to the same old work with the same old clients that don't pay us nearly enough, and aggravate us day after day.

Sometimes we are doing well enough to get by, and the thought of doing something different seems so daunting that we decide it's better to stay exactly where we are. Sometimes we know we want to do something, but we have no idea what to do first, so we wait, hoping it will pop into our heads.

This is angst. This is confusion. It is paralyzing. It is also business-killing, inspiration-murdering behavior.

Inaction bolsters your fear and destroys your confidence. It makes you have more questions and more angst. Inaction keeps you frozen in place.

So why are there some people who always seem to effortlessly accomplish everything?

They know the secret of momentum. It's about action—the act of doing something. It's about getting up every day and doing one little thing to move you further down the line. Even something very small and seemingly inconsequential does at least one thing—it creates more action.

Action cures inertia. It's that simple.

If your business is stuck in neutral, if it is floundering or just getting by, you need to take the first step; just one tiny step every day until you are out of the ditch and on the road to achieving your dream.

Action will get you creativity, inspiration, and growth. I promise.

Chapter 9. Do One Small Thing Today

Here's what I want you to do. Do one thing today—just one thing. Take the quiz on the next page. That's all. That is your inertia-busting assignment for the day.

Think about the questions. Figure out who you really are and what kind of entrepreneur you want to be. Are you a Growth Maven or a Lifestyle Guru?

No need to write a whole business plan that only you and your mother will read. Just picture yourself having the perfect business—what does it look like? How are you living your life?

This is the first step toward having a completely different business in less than 100 days.

Chapter 10. Your Assignment for Day 1: What Kind of Homebased Entrepreneur Are You? A Quiz

You probably have some idea whether you are a Growth Maven or a Lifestyle Guru, but if you are sitting on the fence and not sure in which direction you'd like to go, then this quiz should help you figure that out.

The Quiz

1. When you fantasize about your successful business, what scenario appeals to you the most?

A. More than $500,000 a year in compensation, many employees, a nice office space buzzing with activity, and the knowledge that you are building a well-known regional or national company and brand.

B. A steady low six-figure income, great clients (that you can pick and choose) with challenging and reputation-building projects, and a casual and relaxed environment with plenty of extra time for leisure, home responsibilities, and family.

2. When you think about the perfect workday, which description is more in line with your way of thinking?

A. A cup of Starbucks coffee to get you going, in the office by 8 A.M., eat lunch at a fancy restaurant with prospective clients, high-powered afternoon meetings with investment bankers and members of the media, a strategic planning session with your senior staff, complete employee reviews until 7:30 P.M., meet with colleagues for networking and drinks, get home by 11 P.M.

B. Up at 8 A.M., get kids off to school, at your desk in the spare bedroom working in your sweats until noon, grab a cold burrito from the fridge, conference call with clients while throwing a load into the washer, pick kids up at school at 3 P.M., coach soccer, finish new client proposal, and send invoices. Spouse and kids home at 7:30 for dinner, check e-mail, do 12 little things that need to get done, call Singapore, in bed by 11 P.M.

3. What is your definition of professional success?

A. Building a major business with a legacy, respect of colleagues, financial independence, opportunities to use your position and wealth to make a difference in the
world.

B. Independence, challenging and creative work, time with family and friends, a se-
cure and consistent living, service in the community.

4. I am more comfortable in a working environment that is _____.

A. Formal. I prefer designated spaces for employees, clear boundaries between staff
and management, a conference room for meetings, a receptionist to greet guests,
and a clear beginning and end to the workday.

B. Informal. I prefer to multitask, moving between personal and professional obliga-
tions as they come up. I like to work in my pajamas or sweats (except when going
out to meet clients). I prefer a workday schedule that corresponds to the needs of
my family and my clients, even if that means working at odd hours in the middle
of the night or on weekends.

5. What do you think (hope) your business will be like in ten years?

A. My company, its brand, and its products will be recognized as a leader region-
ally/nationally/internationally, have many employees, be positioned for consistent
future growth, and be constantly innovating in new directions.

B. I will have a steady, but not overwhelming stream of challenging work and an impressive reputation. I will make more than a comfortable living and have plenty of
free time to be with family and friends.

Chapter 11. Growth Mavens to the Right;
Lifestyle Gurus to the Left

Okay, so your first assignment is behind you. You probably have a pretty good idea
now which way you want to take your business. If you answered "A" to at least three
of these questions, you are definitely a Growth Maven. If you answered "B" to at least
three out of the five, then you are a Lifestyle Guru.

This is an important step, because you can't get somewhere unless you know where you want to go. It feels good to have a direction.

This is also the place in the book where the Mavens and Gurus walk down different paths. Chapters 12 to 37 are written specifically for Growth Mavens. The information there is specifically designed to help get you moving toward building your very own empire.

The Gurus have their own section; Chapters 38 to 57. This section helps you create a business that will support your lifestyle. Feel free to stick to the sections that interest you or check out the other side.

We all get back on the same page in Chapter 58, where you learn how to get people talking about your business. Remember—keep doing each of the assignments. You need to do one small thing every day to move your business forward.

One hundred days from now, you'll be amazed at how far your business has progressed!

The Wrap-Up: Day 1

There are two things you need to do before moving on from this section:

1. Be clear that you have a Home Office From Hell and are ready to change your business.

2. Take the Quiz: Are you a Lifestyle Guru or a Growth Maven?

Now, you are done for today. Keep reading and start with your second daily task tomorrow. Great job!

WRAP-UP

Part

So You Wanna Be a Contender?

A Primer for Growth Mavens

*"The real secret of success is enthusiasm. Yes, more than
enthusiasm, I would say excitement. I like to see men get excited.
When they get excited they make a success of their lives."*

—Walter Chrysler

Chapter 12. I Wanna Take Over the World! Okay, So How Do I Do That?

Well, first the bad news…

The odds are stacked against you. The National Federation of Independent Business' Education Foundation estimates that over the lifetime of a small business, only 39 percent are truly profitable. Over a ten-year period, more than 64 percent of these businesses will fail.

These are some tough statistics.

So what's the deciding factor that separates the winners from the losers, and what can you do to start shifting the odds in your favor?

Fortunately, there isn't one, huge overriding factor that will determine if you'll end up on "Millionaire's Row" or "Desolation Row." (For the youngsters out there, this is from a Bob Dylan song…Yes, I'm dating myself.) In fact, your odds for success can be greatly enhanced just by following a series of easy but well-planned small steps. Each small step, by itself, might only move you slightly ahead, but over time you'll be amazed at how far you've come.

So what's the very first step all Growth Mavens should take?

Sorry folks—but it's time to grow up, get dressed, and move out.

And that means out of your bedroom (basement, kitchen, garage, whatever) and into a "real" office space. But not just any type of office space…

Chapter 13. Why You Need to Steer Clear of Real Estate Brokers and Most Landlords

When I speak at small business conferences, I call this section of my talk "There Is No Hell Like Being Locked into a Long-Term Lease," because the standard three- to five-year lease that most real estate brokers and landlords want you to sign can be absolutely catastrophic for a small, growing business.

And there's the dichotomy.

While signing a three- to five-year lease could be tantamount to signing your business' death warrant, most successful real estate brokers won't even talk to you if all you want is a small, short-term deal.

Why is that?

It's because their commissions are based on how many square feet you rent and how long you rent the space for. Unless you are looking for an office for at least ten people for three years or longer, don't even waste your time. They're not interested in your little short-term deal—there's just not enough money in it for them. (Trust me, I know, I was a commercial real estate broker for many years!)

And you can also forget about the vast majority of landlords. They have absolutely no desire to cut up their building into teeny, tiny blocks of 100 or 200 square feet to rent to your no-name company for a few months. And even if they did want to, their lenders would go through the roof—they want the landlord to rent large blocks of space to big-name tenants for three to ten years or longer. (Trust me on this one too—I've worked with many landlords throughout my multi-decade real estate career!)

Of course, they will never admit to any of this. But they are businesspeople. They smile a lot and seem to know what's best for you. They'll present some very logical sounding reasons why you really need to sign a long-term lease (e.g., lock in today's "low" rental rates), but you must remember they are not your buddies. They do not necessarily have your best interests at heart.

In some ways they are just like you. They are trying to maximize their time and efforts. It's a lot more efficient, profitable, and prestigious for them to do a few large, long-term deals with big companies rather than dozens and dozens of tiny, short-term deals with no-name companies like yours. (Yes, many brokers and landlords have healthy egos, so don't discount the value of their boasting rights when they sign a big deal with a big company.)

Just remember, they don't know what's best for you—only you do.

Entrepreneur Story: Jack Barnes

 Jack Barnes, a technology entrepreneur from San Diego, knew it was time to take his small business to the next level.

"The last time I had a client meeting, one of the big bosses ended up sitting on a folding chair in the hallway between my bedroom and bathroom. That's when I knew it was time to make the change."

Jack also knew that he was a Growth Maven at heart. He pictured himself with a big windowed office and a staff of computer whiz kids, holding late-night strategy sessions and making elaborate client presentations that really showed off what his talented company could do. That was the dream. He knew he wanted to make the move out of his bedroom.

But knowing it was time to move out of his home office was the easy part. Jack's next decision was one of the costliest of his small business career. He went out and found himself traditional office space—nicely lit, good building, convenient location, lots of room.

He was excited. He signed a three-year lease.

"I thought the future was looking bright, so I hired some of the most talented kids in the industry and put them all in a state-of-the-art office space. It was beautiful! We felt like we could do no wrong."

That is, until it all fell apart. A sudden downturn in business created a cash flow crunch that Jack didn't see coming. Nine months later, he was handing out pink slips to his talented crew and buckling under the weight of his monthly rental payments. He had to keep paying his hefty rent even though 50 percent of his office was empty!

"We weathered the storm and after another six months, I got the company back on track. But if we could have had a flexible office space that allowed us to grow and shrink as we needed without locking us into a long-term commitment, we would have made a much quicker recovery and had fewer sleepless nights."

Chapter 14. Why You Should Never, Ever Sign a Lease Longer Than 12 Months—Part I

Right now, you are working hard and feeling good about your growth. But a lot can happen in a year. Not to be a pessimist, but you might run into trouble and go bust.

Let's assume that (contrary to my advice) you did sign a lease for three years.

If your business starts to struggle after 5, 12, or even 18 months into the lease, you are still legally obligated to continue paying the full rent to the landlord month after month for the entire three-year term—that's almost 1,100 sleepless nights!

And here's the rub: The ongoing rent payments for an office you can no longer use or afford will only put your business in a more precarious situation and make it even harder, if not impossible, for you to turn things around.

If you're lucky, you might be able to sublease your space to someone else, assuming your lease and market conditions permit that. But instead of spending all your time trying to keep your business afloat, you'll be wasting a lot of time and effort dealing with attorneys and brokers.

And what if, after all your valiant efforts, your business still goes under?

As far as your landlord is concerned, you're by no means off the hook since you probably had no choice but to personally guarantee the lease. So now, on top of all of your other problems (like no business, no job, no money), you have a remaining lease obligation of thousands, if not tens of thousands of dollars, hanging over your head.

That's one scenario…

Chapter 15. Why You Should Never, Ever Sign a Lease Longer Than 12 Months—Part II

What if your situation is the opposite and your business is expanding through the roof?

Let's assume again that you did sign a lease for three years—and your business succeeds. Imagine it—you are turning over product so fast you can hardly keep up. You are bringing on new staff like gangbusters. Interns are sharing desks and executives are squished together like sardines in a tin can. Products are piled into the corners and piles of papers are thrust up on top of file cabinets. Orders are coming in so quickly, you barely have staff to manage it.

And one day, your junior partner is sitting on the windowsill drinking a cup of coffee (because there are no chairs available) and says, "Hey! Maybe we should get ourselves a bigger office."

And you think, "Wow! Great idea!"

Until you remember you are only six months into your three-year lease and you realize that you might end up dying in this office.

Sure, you can try to move some of your crew into additional office space nearby, but that kind of split operation can be an organizational nightmare for an expanding company. I've rarely seen it work out well.

What you now have is four walls that cannot be made flexible enough to meet your needs for growth, and an iron-clad lease that will suffocate your business.

This office is going to be like a boa constrictor wrapped around your business. It will continue to squeeze you into all sorts of uncomfortable places until you can finally move... months or even years down the road.

Chapter 16. Short-Term, Ready-to-Use...What?

There is a simple solution to all this and it is a little known concept that I call the "short-term, ready-to-use office space." Not the most eloquent term, but simply put, this is an office you can move right into.

It is fully equipped, furnished, and ready to go. It has high-speed Internet access, phone systems, furniture, fully functional conference rooms, and in many cases a receptionist to answer the phones. And the lease term can be as short as month-to-month.

What a great idea, right? I wonder why your real estate broker never showed you one of these little gems?

As I mentioned before, real estate brokers typically don't show these spaces because there isn't much money to be made in helping you rent 120 square feet for six months. In most cities the commission on that deal would barely cover a nice dinner for two. That means you may never hear about this type of space, and that's a shame because it is the only way to go for most entrepreneurs interested in moving their businesses off the kitchen table.

These office spaces are available in almost every city and offer small businesses the opportunity to "test drive" a real office space. Entrepreneurs can take out leases for one month, three months, six months, or longer.

The point is, you get to decide. Not the real estate broker. Not the landlord. Because only you know what's right for your business and I want you to be in the driver's seat.

There are two kinds of these ready-to-use spaces; let's talk about each.

Chapter 17. Executive Suites—Look Big Even if You're Still Small

The first type of space is an executive suite (also known as an office business center). These are great "starter" offices because they get you out of your den and into a real office without tying you down with a long-term lease and large up-front capital investments.

Here's how it works. An executive suite company typically rents an entire floor or two in a well-located office building. These buildings tend to be first class, prestigious, and in the heart of the business district. The company then subdivides the space into a large number of offices for rent to individual businesses like yours. These individual offices range in size from about 100 square feet—good for one person—to several hundred square feet—good for up to five people or more.

These suites come with all the amenities. You get top-of-the-line office equipment, telephone and voicemail, videoconferencing, and high-speed Internet access. Executive suites typically offer the very best and latest in technology.

The suites are well dressed—carpeted and typically furnished, from the chairs in the waiting room to the empty file cabinets waiting to be filled. Very often, a receptionist is included in your rent. Secretarial and other administrative services are also available to you on an as-needed basis, so you only pay for those services when you use them. No need to take the time or make the commitment to hire a full-time secretary.

Executive suites are the best option for what I like to call "image" entrepreneurs. These are the folks who know that having a high-end professional appearance will help build their business. They know that looks count. And they know that clients want to place their trust and their business in the hands of someone who walks the walk.

That means they not only have to do great work, but they have to look like they do great work. These entrepreneurs realize that perception is reality—you are only as big as you look. They want to land the big fish clients and compete with companies many times their size. And this is how they do it.

Imagine moving your business out of your basement and into a state-of-the-art executive suite. Imagine prospective clients coming to see you in your gorgeous office where they are greeted by a friendly receptionist and given coffee while they wait in comfy chairs. Then imagine these prospective clients being blown away by your high-tech-enabled presentation and the videoconferencing you did with your partner in London.

Much better than making your presentation in your living room next to the wet socks hanging off the TV set, right?

Chapter 18. More about Looking (and Thinking) Big Even if You're Still Small

I want you to be the maverick that you always wanted to be.

So no matter how bleak your home office situation, know that you can change it fast. Know that in as little as a single day—yes, a single day—you can get yourself an affordable office and start down the path to becoming a real Growth Maven.

That's right! It can happen that quickly! No lengthy lease agreements. No protracted negotiations. No attorney fees. No meddling brokers. Just put on some pants, lock your front door, and make the move. I give you all the information you need at the end of this section.

If you're already sold, skip to Chapter 29 for your Week One Assignments. Still not sure? Here are six more things you should know about executive suites:

1. No up-front construction or renovation costs.

Nor is there a need to buy office equipment or furniture. You do not have to run to Staples and load up on swivel chairs and file cabinets. It is all included and that means less financial drain on your growing business.

2. Total flexibility in the length of your lease term.

You get to make arrangements based on your business and cash flow needs. You can rent these offices for 6 to 12 months at a time, which is the usual rental agreement. Or you can even go shorter term. Many executive suites will rent for a lease term as short as 3 months or even on a month-to-month basis. This feature is especially attractive to entrepreneurs who are just getting their businesses up and running and don't want to strap the business with a huge overhead at the onset.

3. Downsize or expand on demand.

If your business expands, you can rent more space. If you need to downsize on short notice, you can alter your agreement. If you are in an industry that expands and contracts seasonally or in cycles, this is a great option that helps you be more in control of your cash flow.

4. Manage your cash flow easily.

Take care of every office expense in an all-inclusive monthly bill. This makes your bookkeeping easier. You will get a single invoice every month. Usually it includes everything—heating, air conditioning, electrical, cleaning, telephone, Internet, furniture. This simplifies your renting experience and helps you better manage your cash flow over the long term.

5. Create a clear line of division between work and home.

One of the big benefits of these suites is having clearer boundaries in your life. More organization. Less chaos. When you are at your office, you are focused on work and the day's tasks. When you are home, you can focus your attention on family and your household. The line of division is clear for everyone, most especially you.

6. Get out and network easily.

Sometimes working in your home office means that the only networking you do is with the neighbor's dog. It can be downright lonely working at home and it means you have to be very aggressive about making contact with other people. Executive suites may have as few as a couple dozen companies or as many as a hundred companies housed within their space. That means that potential clients and partners are just a few feet away from your door on any given day. Networking just got a whole lot easier.

Entrepreneur Story: Bob Carter

Bob Carter used to work out of his home office.

"I liked the idea of being my own boss and I had this picture in my head that I would make the 60-second commute to the computer in my socks and spend my day being focused and hyper-productive."

Bob had good intentions. But he found himself distracted by his overgrown lawn, a mile-long "honey-do" list, and his son's geometry homework.

"All these things needed to be done. What is more important? A deadline for a client or helping your kid pass his geometry exam? I was always torn."

Bob called me wanting to know how he could get a "real" office on a shoestring budget—a separate space that he could define as a place to work and make his home a place to play and do home-related chores. But Bob had just gotten his business off the ground and he had limited cash flow. He knew he couldn't handle a large rental commitment and the upfront costs for office equipment and furniture. The task seemed overwhelming to him.

"The more I thought about it, the more I felt paralyzed. I kept doing nothing. And things just went from bad to worse. I was taking client calls at my kid's soccer game and tapping away at my laptop at the breakfast table. I just wasn't present for my family or my clients."

I found Bob a great executive suite just a 12-minute drive from his house. He moved all his files in the back of his SUV (about three trips), so the move cost him less than $40 (for packing tape, boxes, and gas). He didn't have to buy a single piece of office furniture or equipment. He didn't have to run out to Staples once! In fact, he kept his fax machine and a computer at his house, so he could do some work in the evenings after the kids went to bed. He has been in his new suite for the last seven months.

When I checked in with him for this book, he told me, "This is more like what I had imagined for my business. I still work on my own terms and have the flexibility I had imagined when I started my business, but the boundaries are clearer for me and simpler for my family—when I'm at work, I'm at work. When I'm home, I'm home."

Chapter 19. The Fine Print: Okay, There Are Some Downsides . . .

There are downsides to everything and executive suites are no exception.

Downside number 1: Executive suites are almost always located in first-class office buildings. That means they are Class A, more expensive, and in main business districts. That may work beautifully for your business if you are an accountant or an attorney, but maybe not so much if you are a video game designer.

Most of these suites tend to be mainstream, corporate, and traditional. If you are more funky or less image conscious, then an executive suite may not represent you or your business well. Having said that, a number of smart executive suite owners are starting to open centers that are very cool and "downtown" in both design and location.

Downside number 2: If you need space for more than ten people, an executive suite can start getting expensive. If you really think (not hope) that you will have more than ten employees by the end of the year, you might want to look at a different alternative.

Chapter 20. Shared Office Space: A Place for "Funky" Entrepreneurs

We often use the word "entrepreneur" to name a single group of driven, independent, self-disciplined people who are looking to make their own place in the business world. But the truth is, entrepreneurs are not so easily categorized. They come in as many different flavors as Ben and Jerry's. I constantly remind myself that not every entrepreneur wants or is suitable for the same type of office space.

Take Jake Martin, for example. He is a theater producer in New York and needed a low-cost space with a short lease that would help him manage the cyclical nature of New York theater. He didn't want to get stuck with a pricey office if his shows started losing money and he needed to downsize, but he also knew that if he was producing several shows at once, the size of his staff could increase substantially. He needed flexibility…but he also needed something else.

Jake was a creative guy in a creative business. His shows were cutting edge and so he needed to be seen that way, too. He was young, wore his hair long, biked to work, and preferred t-shirts and designer jeans to suits.

Jake hated the executive suites.

"Too stuffy, too investment banker…" he said to me. "We aren't cubicle people on Madison Avenue."

This is where shared office space comes in. Shared spaces give you many of the same benefits as the executive suites, but if you work in a nontraditional business or just plain see yourself as a "funky entrepreneur," then these might be the best option for your biz.

Check it out…

Chapter 21. The Lowdown on Shared Office Space

Sharing space is an excellent alternative for people who are looking for more off-beat locations or a more casual aesthetic.

Shared office space is nothing more than subleasing a part of someone else's office—a simple concept. And there are even more shared spaces than executive suites available throughout the United States. While there are some 3,000 individual executive suite locations throughout the United States, there are hundreds of thousands of shared office space opportunities, from the largest cities to the smallest towns.

Many companies are looking to rent their excess space to budding entrepreneurs. Maybe they downsized, or maybe they rented extra space for future growth and don't need it yet. For whatever reason, they need tenants and are willing to share their resources. This is great news for entrepreneurs like Jake.

Getting out of your home office cave also means finding new ways to meet and work with new colleagues. Jake, for instance, moved his theater production business into a shared space with a rock promoter and an entertainment lawyer. Not only did they all have the same desire to create a casual business environment in their funky downtown loft, but Jake hired the entertainment lawyer and is producing a show at Carnegie Hall next year with the rock promoter.

The arrangement has worked fantastically for all of them.

Chapter 22. Create Your Ideal Office Culture and Send a Message about You and Your Company

What you get with shared office space is the opportunity to create the office that best fits you, your style, and your business. It allows you to create the office culture that speaks accurately about who you are and what you believe in.

Want to give your employees a break with a little foosball over lunch? Shared space. Want to bring your chihuahua to work? Shared space. Maybe you want to open an animation studio in an old, restored canning factory? You get the idea. You can choose the perfect environment to grow your business. You have an almost infinite supply of choices in front of you.

Sharing space also allows you to network and share resources—an added bonus. Many companies are excited to rent to a complementary business. Your jewelry design business might really benefit from that advertising agency just next door, and who knows how that accountant could end up saving you thousands of dollars in taxes next year. Shared space is also great if you are not a natural networker. It is a natural and comfortable way to meet people and make connections.

Chapter 23. You're Not Alone Anymore!

"The best thing about getting out of my home office is that I now have on-site networking…and I don't have to leave my desk to do it," Maria said, talking to me from the hip downtown Manhattan office space she shares with six other companies. "We've really maximized our relationships right here in the office."

This was exciting for me to hear—that people who shared offices put their entrepreneurial experience to work and networked right at their desks.

I was so excited by this that I called many of my clients who were in shared spaces and executive suites and I asked them about this very thing: In what creative ways have you used your shared office environment to improve your business and networking?

I had no idea what to expect. Maybe Maria's experience was unique, a product of her charismatic personality and her will to succeed. But what I found is that entrepreneurs are using their ambition and networking skills to maximize their client lists right in their own offices.

The very idea of sharing space either as a subtenant or in an executive suite means that you are in the world, connecting to and interacting with other people. Because of this simple change in logistics, you are not locked away in your home office with only Oprah and Dr. Phil to keep you company.

You almost *need* to network. We are social animals after all, and we are pulled by our pack nature to be with other folks. Feeling shy about getting started? No worries. A few highly motivated entrepreneurs have put together their favorite ways to make connections at the desk next door.

Chapter 24. The Things That Can Happen When You Leave Your Home Office Cave Behind...

So, how can you maximize the relationships you have right around you in your office space? I asked my clients—in both shared spaces and executive suites—that very question. These are some of the best tips they offered. Each is based on my clients' own personal experience of how they created meaningful relationships that improved their business.

Throw a party.

There's nothing like an office party and a few cups (only a few) of punch to break down walls and create long-lasting partnerships. The next time you are thinking about having a little post-work soirée or lunchtime gathering, invite your officemates. They will appreciate the gesture and everyone will get to know each other better.

Janet told me she set up a fancy breakfast the week she moved her tiny law firm into her executive suite and invited everyone to the conference room for coffee and a continental breakfast.

"I was kind of intimidated. The people around us were very established and we were this struggling, fledgling firm."

But the breakfast she hosted was not only an act of bravery, it successfully broke the ice and enhanced her business.

"I got a chance to talk about what we really did. Now, one of the larger and established law firms sends us referrals for clients who are too small for their business. It's worked out great for both of us," she said.

"Just having a few minutes to really talk about our business in an informal setting was great for our business."

There is no substitute for a clear and specific invitation.

Rick tried to create a similar kind of event in his shared space in San Francisco. He hosted an after-work cocktail hour and invited everyone in the office, roughly 30 people. "It was a mess…I put up a notice on the kitchen bulletin board and thought the place would fill up by 7 P.M. I bought tons of food and made margaritas. Only six people came. I was embarrassed." Rick confessed.

The experience was so disappointing, he vowed to never host another party again. But I asked him to try it again, only this time to ask everyone personally. He was apprehensive but he tried it.

"I made an invitation on my computer with details about the party. I used the title "Jacobs-Evers wants to get to know their new officemates—Come have a drink with us!" Rick explained.

"…and I personally hand-delivered the invite to each desk."

Turns out many of the people in the office hadn't even looked at the bulletin board and were oblivious to the previous party. By creating a party with a networking purpose and hand-delivering the invitation to every person, Rick gave the party a personal touch. He also had an excuse to talk to everyone in the office and get to know their names.

"Second time's a charm." Rick told me shortly after.

"The party lasted until 2 A.M. and I think we discovered some interesting ways to work together in the future."

Don't assume people will respond to a half-hearted or unstructured invite. People need boundaries and they don't want to feel awkward walking into an unknown environment. People need reassurance that they are wanted at the event. The more specific the invitation, the more comfortable people will feel and the more they will respond.

Be generous—good deeds beget more good deeds.

A good way to connect with people is to do something nice. A favor, a phone call, or a referral can go a long way toward creating a strong working relationship.

If the business next to you needs to buy a new laptop and you know someone who can get them a discount, make a phone call. If you are not going to take on a potential client but you feel comfortable making a referral to your officemate, do it. If your little sister can sub as a receptionist while your office neighbor looks for a replacement, offer it and make it happen.

These little gestures often take minutes of your time but they can have a lasting impact with people just getting to know you. Don't waste an opportunity to show people what kind of person you are and what kind of business you run.

Phil helped his officemate after meeting him only once in the hallway.

"He had a huge deadline and was down two staff people. I had been there more than once, so I loaned him some of my assistants for three days and it made all the difference."

That single act was the basis for years of friendship and work together. Crisis is always an opportunity for you to show people what you're made of.

Don't be a nuisance.

Boundaries are everything. Yes, you should reach out to the people around you. And yes, you should try to make complementary business connections. But if people aren't biting, you shouldn't keep pushing.

"I wasn't picking up on the signals," Russ confided to me.

"All I wanted was to see if I could get the company next to me to make an introduction. They seemed very pleasant about it at first, but I stayed on them and finally, the director took me aside and told me I should 'let it go.' The relationship was never the same after that."

The thing that makes you a great entrepreneur—drive, tenacity, the ability to bypass "no"—can also make you a predator in the closed space of an office. Make sure you are creating and responding to boundaries—90 percent of our communication is nonverbal, so look for the cues and take them to heart. If you feel a little resistance, back off.

Take a second look.

You may not think the guy in the next office plugging away on his computer has anything to do with you or your business, but you might be wrong.

Wendy, a marketing consultant in the fashion industry, barely spoke to Wayne, who shared her office.

"He was always hunched over his computer, doing something complicated with numbers and figures. It never occurred to me his business would have anything in common with my business," Wendy said.

It turns out Wayne was a financial planner for some very big fashion clients.

"We got to talking in the office kitchen and really hit it off. Then we realized we worked primarily in the same industry. It was incredible! That week, I started introducing my clients to him and he started introducing his clients to me."

Sometimes we just don't give someone a second look. They might be shy, aloof, or involved in a business that seems completely different than ours, but there is always a benefit to looking deeper—to being curious and interested in people around us.

You never know what you might find in your new office! A long-lasting partnership, a lifelong friendship, a good vibe in your office, better clients, a healthier business, a more fulfilled life...who knows!

Just get out of your home office dungeon—the possibilities out there are endless.

Chapter 25. The "I'm Feelin' Kinda Funky" Checklist

Are you feeling funky? Are you ready to bring your chihuahua, Horatio, to work every day? Are you ready to do some real networking? Do you think sharing a space might be the best way to jump in to your first "real" office? If so, here are some important things to consider before you pack up Horatio in his crate.

Location! Location! Location!

The old real estate mantra applies here, too. If you need to have clients in frequently, or you want to have a location close to your vendors, then limit your search criteria to the most desirable locations.

You should be thinking about how easy it is for clients and employees to park their cars or take public transportation. Never give a client a reason to say "no" to coming to your office. You want every possible opportunity to show these guys who you are and how great your company is.

If proximity isn't as important, you can save money by moving to a more out-of-the-way location. But think—how will employees get to your office? Sure, renting an office on the outskirts of town, way out by the airport, might be cost effective, but you might never be able to attract great candidates. Weigh these issues against the cost.

Hold out for the "Big Seven" office features.

Shared spaces can come with lots of amenities or just a few, so look closely and think carefully about what features are most important to you.

The "Big Seven" services that might be available are (1) Business equipment such as faxes and copiers, (2) Receptionist/personalized telephone answering, (3) Office furniture (desks, chairs, etc.), (4) Reception area for visitors, (5) Use of kitchen, (6) Use of conference room(s), and (7) Signage on the door and elsewhere.

There might be a few others, like a gym or restaurant on the premises, but you should have an idea about what you expect from them regarding the Big Seven.

Does the company seem stable and legal?

You want stability for your business, so if a host company is fragile, in danger of losing their lease, or hemorrhaging money, you want to go somewhere else. You can't be a mind reader, so do some research. Ask people in their industry about them or do a simple Internet search. Know how long they have been in the space and whether they have moved around a lot. Ask questions.

Transparency is the key here, and your gut reaction will almost always be right. If they give you rational and specific answers, that is a good sign. Too much hype without substance or shadowy information is a sign to turn tail. Trust yourself and think first about what is good for your business.

Check the legal stuff.

Is this a lease for three months or the next five years? Make sure you read the lease carefully and don't assume they are all the same. Read the fine print. Make sure all the amenities you have been promised are written into the contract.

For executive suites: Ask about additional charges—phone, Internet, administrative, parking, after-hour access, air conditioning, electricity, cleaning, etc. What are the upfront charges? Security deposit, first month's/last month's rent, credit check, etc.? Then get a copy of the agreement. Many executive suites have gone with a relatively simple plain English two- or three-page agreement that you can sit and read in about 20 minutes. If it's much longer than six or seven pages, then take it home and read it there or send it to your attorney.

Don't be pressured into signing on the spot. If you want to reserve your space, have them charge a nominal and refundable deposit (like $100) to your credit card. That should easily buy you a couple of days to have the contract reviewed. Remember, you should only be committing to a maximum of 6 to 12 months at a time so you probably can't screw up too badly. (This is not legal advice—to avoid potential problems you should always have your contracts reviewed by an attorney.)

For shared office space: This is a bit more complicated. Since this is technically a sublease, you need to have your attorney review the sublease agreement. Your attorney also needs to review the main (master) lease between the company you are subleasing from and their landlord. He needs to make sure that they have the right to sublease, and if there are any onerous provisions in their lease that can cause you problems.

In almost every case, the landlord must approve any sublease. Your potential officemates do not want to provide a written sublease agreement? They refuse to give you a copy of their main lease? (They can always black out the financial information, such as the amount of rent they're paying, but other than that you need to see all the other provisions of their lease.) Or do they tell you not to worry about it—the landlord doesn't need to approve the lease? Any of these is a major warning sign.

Resist the pressure!

Take your time and find the best deal with the best features for your business. Don't let anyone pressure you with stories about this "one of a kind space going quickly." Never give in to pushy tactics to get you to close the deal quickly without looking at the details of the space and the contract.

Only you know what is best for your business!

Chapter 26. A Small Disclaimer to Remember When You Share Office Space

Not every example of space sharing will end the way it did for Jake, in pure bliss. But most can do well, if you keep in mind that shared office spaces are not managed by professionals. Where executive suites are run by a company solely devoted to meeting your small-office needs, shared spaces are run by the people who inhabit them—accountants, artists, designers, just like you.

They are regular folks and, as such, they may or may not be great landlords. The copier might always be on the fritz and the receptionist might smack her gum too loudly. You also might be dealing with an officemate who plays Metallica at full blast or likes to give himself a pedicure at his desk in the middle of the afternoon.

This is all part of the unpredictability of moving in with strangers, but if you are up for the ride, you could find a match made in office heaven!

Chapter 27. The Devil's in the Details

My mother used to say that you can tell a lot about a restaurant by checking out the bathrooms. Her theory was that when a business pays attention to making the restrooms comfortable and clean, they probably put similar energy into the food and the service.

Mark my words, that woman would walk into a restaurant and march right to the restroom for an inspection before ordering. If the bathroom was a mess, she was out of there. She knew the value of the details.

It is no different with shared office space or executive suites. No matter what the hype, you will want to look at the little things to ensure your potential officemates are right for you and your business.

You are not only looking for a great office space, but also a great partner, a business that complements your work habits and style. Choose the right one and you have a match made in heaven. Choose wrong and, well, you've just moved into The Shared Office From Hell!

Who needs that?

It's crucial you get in bed with the right people. Remember, you are interviewing them as much as they are interviewing you. Be observant and maybe even downright paranoid. Look in the corners. Keep your eye on the little things. Check out the bathrooms before you order the food!

Here are my eight tips to help you find the perfect officemate:

1. Think clean!

Take a good, thorough look at the office. Are the bathrooms scrubbed? Are the waste baskets emptied and the carpets vacuumed? What does the carpet look like—is it worn and/or stained? Has the refrigerator been cleaned out in the last week or does it look more like a science experiment? This office is going to speak for you. Make sure it sends the right message to your clients.

2. Check out the culture.

Who are the people with whom you will spend 40 to 60 hours a week in this office? Ask them about their business, their hours, their clients, and how they run their business. You might raise an eyebrow or two if one of their clients is the Hell's Angels! Find out if you will have complete access to the conference room or if you will be put on a schedule. Look at what they are wearing, how they interact with each other. Be aware. Take an interest in them. Then, imagine your business in the space. If you can't see yourself there, it's not the right place for you.

3. Make a special note of the things that could drive you crazy.

Thinking ahead will help you stave off potential problems. What is important to you? What about your new officemate might prove annoying or challenging for your business? If the office is loud and raucous, but you need quiet to get your business done, this may not be the space for you. Make a list of everything you need and make sure this situation will enable you to get it.

4. Details! Details!

Does the receptionist have tattoos and tongue piercings, and is that in line with your company's image? Are your potential officemates friendly and professional to strangers? The little things say a lot about your business, so you need to be looking at the minutiae now, before you move in.

5. Make small talk when the boss isn't around.

Everyone loves to talk and be listened to. So listen. Strike up conversations with assistants and receptionists. They are good sources to get the real deal on a company. Start up a conversation and see what you learn!

6. Ask to see the exact office you will be renting.

Does it have a window or is it an interior office? Does it offer the privacy you need? Is the access to your office workable? What furniture is included in your rent? How much conference room time is included in your monthly rent? How many conference rooms do they have? You want to make sure that they have several depending on how many other businesses they house.

7. Catch the vibe.

How does the office feel? Do you feel tense as soon as you walk in? Are people smiling and working together in groups? Is the boss screaming at the employees? Do the employees seem serious about their work or are they more intent on goofing off? Their vibe needs to jive with your vibe. Take a second to step back and see how you feel when you are in the office. If you want to flee, then do it!

8. Imagine your dream client in the space.

You know who your clients are and what is important to them. More importantly, you know who you want your next clients to be. Picture your dream client coming in to your office to meet you. Is this the kind of office that underscores who you are? Can you make a great impression here? Will your corporate clients think your office is too "downtown" or will they see you as more creative than your corporate counterparts? Is there anything about this office that might make it hard to bring in new clients? If you can picture making a great impression with clients and accomplishing some excellent work, you may have a match made in heaven!

Entrepreneur Story: Eileen Kelly

 Eileen Kelly is a client of mine and a graphic designer from Phoenix, Arizona.

She thought she was making a great choice by sharing a cool space with a young Internet advertising start-up.

"I thought I might get some work out of the relationship and meet new contacts," she told me.

Turns out, the company was poorly managed by an absentee boss and the employees were not nearly as serious about their work as Eileen. Their disruptive work habits started to interfere with Eileen's business.

"The guys had a late night strategy session the night before I had a big presentation for a new client. The meeting must have gone long and they ordered pizza and beer. Problem is, they left the conference room and kitchen a complete mess and the meeting room smelled like stale beer," Eileen explained.

"Instead of going over my client presentation, I spent the morning scouring the office. I got the client, but I realized I had moved in with the wrong team. We just didn't share the same values."

And that says it all. If you are going to share space, you need to find office mates who share your values and complement your business.

Remember, you are interviewing them as much as they are interviewing you. Ask the right questions. Don't be intimidated. And listen to your gut. If the space feels wrong—even if you can't figure out why—run!

Chapter 28. Still Need More Reasons to Make the Move Out of Your Home Office From Hell? Here Are Seven!

Reason number 7: Your grandmother would like the spare bedroom back.

Reason number 6: The neighbors are starting to think you *really are* unemployed.

Reason number 5: Your clients are worried you'll dump them as soon as you get a real job.

Reason number 4: Your competitors have counted you out of the game—or worse, they have never even heard of you.

Reason number 3: There are some great office space alternatives out there that will not break the bank, but will help you look bigger and more impressive.

Reason number 2: Making the leap is not nearly as scary as it first seemed and if you follow this week's assignment, you could be in "real" office space by next week and on your way to becoming the tycoon you always knew you could be.

Reason number 1: You are a Growth Maven at heart. You must now get out of your pajamas if you are going to conquer the world!

Enough said!

Chapter 29. Getting Your Real Office: Your Assignments for Days 2–6

I'm giving you five days to find your new office space—either an executive suite or shared office space. Here are the steps:

Day 2: OK, the first thing you need to do is figure out how to find all the available executive suites and shared office space located in your geographic area of interest. You can attack this a couple of ways: (1) You can search the classified real estate sections of your local newspapers, look through the Yellow Pages, do a Google search, or scroll through the listings on Craigslist. All of these will get you to office space options. Or (2) You can go right to Offices2Share.com and you'll get all the information you need in one place. (More on that in a moment.)

Day 3: Once you've completed your search and narrowed down your list of executive suites and/or shared office spaces in your preferred locations, start calling them to find out what spaces are available, their asking prices, what's included in the rent, if there are additional charges, and so on.

Day 4: Narrow down your list to no more than your five top choices and make an appointment to tour each location.

Day 5: Visit all five locations. You should be able to complete this in one day. Conduct the same type of due diligence that you would use if you were looking to rent an apartment. Go back to the checklists and make a list of questions to ask, things to look for, etc. Decide what is important to you and do not deviate from the plan.

Day 6: Sign the agreement and pay any up-front fees (security deposit, etc.). Plan to make the move.

Now, this is where I tell you that I, in fact, own Offices2Share.com, so using our services will put a small amount of money in my pocket (paid for by the executive suite owner or the shared office space owner, *not* by you) and you will be contributing to my lifestyle, my wife's sense of well-being in the world, and my kids' college education. You do not have to use our company to get yourself into an office, but if you do, know that we started this site for the express purpose of helping entrepreneurs like you get their start as easily and as cheaply as possible. So check us out. If you like us, use us. If not, use another option, but one way or the other…get out of your Home Office From Hell!

Chapter 30. Organizing the Move: Nine Do's and Don'ts for Cost-Effective, Low-Hassle Moving

1. **Get rid of dead files and other useless items before the move.** No reason to clutter the new office with stuff you'll rarely or never use! Anyway, holding on to useless stuff is a psychological barrier to getting a new start. If you're really not sure, then leave it at home for the time being.

2. **Send out some form of communication (e-mails, cards, postcards, etc.— whatever is appropriate for your business) alerting colleagues of your new contact info.** Remember, this move is also a great opportunity to speak to or reconnect with old clients. Don't be afraid to use the move as a reason to get back in touch and let people know about your new services and products. Even better, use this move as an excuse to get some PR (local newspaper, industry magazine, or local radio, for example). You can say things like, "Our business has been expanding so quickly we needed to move into larger quarters."

3. **Order preprinted address labels with your new address as soon as you know what it will be.** This makes the change-of-address process much easier. Throw away outdated brochures, business cards, and other inexpensive paraphernalia with your old contact information. To save money, use the new address labels over the old address on brochures and other expensive promotional materials. Just make sure it doesn't look shoddy.

4. **Since you won't be toting lots of furniture, consider making the move with a borrowed pick-up truck and a friend or two.** Take everyone out to a diner afterward and you've saved yourself some money on a U-Haul truck.

5. **As you pack, mark each box with its contents and keep a box count and a master list, so you know what stuff is in which box.** You never know when a client will have an emergency and you don't want to be digging through boxes to find the paperwork you need. Put all business essentials in one "Top Priority" box.

6. **File an official change of business address with the post office.** You can do it quite easily at: www.usps.com.

7. **Make arrangements ahead of time so that all Internet access and phones will be available on your move-in date.** You'll want to plug in and set up shop as soon as you get there.

8. **Check out obstacles to the move in advance.** Are there flights of stairs or elevators? Are the streets narrow or wide? Can you double park, or arrange with the building manager for special parking permission during your move?

9. **Once you get there, set up a staging area.** Pull your essentials out of your "Top Priority" box and get one area up and running with some functionality. That way some essential business can be conducted while the rest of the unpacking is being done.

Get a Phone Number to Go...

Before you move to your new office, make arrangements with the phone company to get a portable phone number with a prestigious area code (like a 212 number in Manhattan) with call forwarding.

This is the number you should use on all your stationery, business cards, and marketing material—not the phone number that you get from the executive suite or your new shared office. Here's why:

If you move in the future to another office location, you get to keep this number (which is the number that all of your clients, vendors, friends, and family know). Just forward it to the new office phone number. And if you run into trouble and need to go back to your home office, you can keep the prestigious number and have the calls forwarded to your home phone.

Your clients will never know that you're back in your house in Long Island, unless, of course, they try to visit you!

Chapter 31. Making the Move: Your Assignments for Days 7–13

Moving is stressful and never fun, so plan ahead, make lists, and plan for emergencies. Now that you have your new office, you should start making the move. It should take you no more than a week to organize and complete.

Day 7: Contact the U.S. Postal Service and make a business address change. Get boxes from a local store or buy them new from a stationery store. Make sure all the office paperwork is in order.

Day 8: Decide whether you will be using a professional mover, U-Haul truck, or a personal vehicle. Make arrangements with people who will help you move and decide how you will re-pay them for their help (dinner at a local diner, for example).

Day 9: Start packing up nonessential business items: files, folders, paper, etc. Mark each box with a clear description and make a list of supplies you will need for the new office.

Day 10: Send out communication to businesses about your intentions to move. Get together all of the phone numbers you will need for the move day (people who are helping, movers, office manager, doorman, local restaurants, etc.).

Day 11: Shop for new supplies and pack more nonessential business items. Check with office manager to confirm move-in time and any last-minute instructions. Confirm that the phone and Internet have been turned on.

Day 12: Do the last important business that needs to be done. Pack all the essential business items into a "Top Priority" box that will be set up immediately once you get into the new office. Call helpers and have them meet at a single place at a specific time and let them know the plan for the move (who will go in what vehicle, what each will be responsible for, and so on). Get a handful of petty cash to tip various people.

Day 13: Moving Day! Give everyone a task and set them to work. Set up the staging area while boxes are being moved in.

Chapter 32. You Are the Captain!

Finally, you're sitting at your desk in your cool new office with the short lease and you're pretty proud of yourself, but you're thinking, "Okay, so here I am. I'm ready to start empire building...now what?"

And that's a really good question, because even though the walls look new and the view from the window is different, the business is still the same. You still need to get more and better clients and start making more money. And not only that, you really want more time with your family and friends.

I'm sure you're probably wondering how in the world you'll be able to pull any of that off when you couldn't do it before with only a 30-second commute to your basement office.

Well, I'm going to take you through the steps to get there, but first you need to streamline.

Streamline...sounds easy enough, right? It is.

You need to decide which of your daily jobs are revenue-producing and which are non-revenue-producing time-suckers. Revenue-producing jobs are the jobs that help you build the business. They consist of creating a vision for the company, getting the word out to prospective clients about your business, negotiating joint ventures, creating new products and services, and so on.

Time-sucking jobs come in two varieties: (1) Professional types of jobs, such as accounting, advertising, bookkeeping, legal, website design, etc., and (2) Administrative jobs, such as appointment-setting, data entry, filing, invoicing, order processing, etc.

As important as these jobs are in the proper functioning of any business, Growth Mavens do not personally do them. Your job is to grow and promote your company. You need to create new products and services and get them out to customers. Anything else is not a productive use of your time.

So keep the ship steered toward your vision. You are the Captain. I want the crew to tidy the deck and lift the mast.

Chapter 33. Staff? I Can't Afford to Hire Staff!

Really? I think you can't afford *not* to hire staff.

Think of it this way—how much is your time worth per hour? If you live in a good-sized American city or town doing highly skilled work, you might be worth anywhere from $100 to $600 per hour.

Give yourself an hourly rate. How much do you think your time and skills are worth on the open market?

Now, think about what you did today…filing and sending out invoices, attending to your schedule, making flight reservations, arguing with the hotel clerk, checking in with vendors, dumping the wastebaskets…everything, right? So, if your time is worth $200 per hour and you spent one hour of your day filing and sending out invoices, it's the same as paying someone else $200 to do that work.

Would you pay someone $200 per hour to file and send out invoices?

Of course not!

But you just did. Imagine instead that you spent that hour developing a new product or service or setting up a new joint venture. Or putting into motion a great plan to get your company out there and noticed by potential customers. That is work worth $200 per hour.

See what I mean? You can't afford to keep paying yourself $200 per hour to do the lower-level, non-revenue-producing grunt work. It will kill your business and ruin your personal life.

What you need is inexpensive, reliable, knowledgeable help. And I have just the answer.

Chapter 34. Hire Just One Perfect Person

Forget hiring an entire army of staff for right now. I want you to bring on just one person.

Your mind is going crazy, right? Already you are flipping from scenario to complicated scenario—want ads, résumés, interviews, call-backs, lengthy orientations, negotiations, workman's comp, taxes, more of your precious money out the window…argh!

This is the stuff that creates clutter in your head and prevents you from moving your business forward. I want to make bringing on a staff person as easy as possible with no long-term commitments and little or no up-front costs—sort of like the human version of short-term, ready-to-use office space!

So, I'm giving you one simple solution, a crazy idea called a "virtual assistant," or VA.

Sounds kind of weird, right? Well, a VA is a great first hire for Growth Mavens because they provide a low-commitment, low-cost solution that can free you to do the important business-growing jobs that are essential to building your empire.

Not only that, VAs are small business owners themselves, so they completely understand the entrepreneurial mindset. You want someone who can empathize with your daily challenges, and knows firsthand the importance of providing great customer service.

The VA works off-site (typically from their own home office), so you don't have to pay for employee benefits, payroll taxes, office supplies, vacation, etc. They provide their own supplies and equipment. You pay them hourly and they only work the hours you need them. That means if you have two hours of telephone calls to return, data entry, and creating sales reports, you only pay for those two hours.

The VAs are pros and many of them have specialized skills, such as bookkeeping, web design, and ghostwriting. And if you use a virtual staffing agency (similar to a temp agency), you'll be assigned a project manager who will work with you to find the right VA or combination of VAs to get your various jobs done.

With a virtual staffing agency there's no need to review resumes, interview candidates, etc.—your project manager will handle all of that for you. And if you don't love your VA you can always trade him or her for another one.

There are no pesky personal problems or issues, just a clear mandate to get work done that is a drain on your time and ability to be a Growth Maven.

What Can a VA Do for You?

You should already be compiling a list of time-sucking, energy-robbing jobs that you can't wait to hand off to your VA starting tomorrow. If you're having trouble, this list should get you started:

- *Creating and maintaining your mailing list*
- *Responding to customer calls and e-mails*
- *Responding to comments on your blog*
- *Putting together your weekly/monthly schedule*
- *Scheduling and coordinating meetings, appointments (professional and personal), and interviews*
- *Researching business trips, vacations, and travel destinations*
- *Booking hotels and flights*
- *Researching competitors, potential partners, vendors, and clients on the Internet*
- *Bookkeeping and light accounting, including paying bills, data entry into QuickBooks, expense reports, etc.*
- *Making changes to your blog or website and working with your web person (if you have one)*
- *Managing shipping and distribution of your products*
- *Arranging speaking opportunities (read the rest of the book and you'll know why this is important!)*
- *Sending articles and columns off to various magazine editors (this one, too!)*
- *Designing presentations*

This list can really be as long as your imagination and your business needs, but you get the idea. These jobs are crucial but they will also soak up all the time and energy out of your day. Either you won't get the important Growth Maven–visionary work done, or you will be pounding the computer at 2 A.M. Neither is good for you or your business.

No one ever built an empire all by himself or herself, and you can't either!

Chapter 35. As with Everything, the Drawbacks...

Sounds like heaven, right?

If only VAs were perfect, but alas, they are not. Here are a few things to keep in mind:

- VAs typically cost $30 or more per hour (depending on where they're based and if you require specialized skills). Sounds astronomical but you will have no outside expenses (taxes and benefits) and you are only paying for the hours they actually work, so your VA will not be costing you while they're out having lunch, on vacation, or out sick.
- VAs are not well suited for last-minute projects. You should be able to think about what needs to be done on a consistent and ongoing basis and create a set list of projects for them to complete. You can't throw last-minute things at VAs. Since VAs have other clients besides you, they may not be able to accommodate last-minute or urgent requests and if they can, it might be at a premium rate.
- You have to get organized to use VAs effectively. They are best used for specific and ongoing tasks. "Research snowboarding in the Alps." "Create a flow chart." "Update the invoices." They work best with concrete and specific tasks, so get clear about what you want and make the instructions clear.
- It is possible to get a bum VA, but you can speak to your project manager and have a new one assigned to you (if you use a virtual staffing agency).

Using a VA will help you learn to delegate and create clear instructions. Also, remember to think about what your expectations are for your VA. When you speak to the project manager, make sure you tell him what kind of person you are looking for—the qualities and skills that are important to you.

You want to set this up for success right from the start.

Entrepreneur Story: Eva Siitonen

My friend Eva started her business because she loves—I mean really loves—jewelry.

"I have loved baubles and beads from the earliest time I can remember. I was probably four when I first begged my mom to take me to Deco-World and buy plastic beads so I could string them together and make necklaces and bracelets for every member of the family—even my dad!"

This passion for making jewelry stayed with her and by the time she was out of college with her art degree, her talent for making unusual pieces of jewelry had caught the attention of everyone from college kids to socialites.

"It was exciting when I realized my passion could be my career."

But Eva was more of an artist than an entrepreneur.

"I loved actually designing and creating the pieces but I didn't have a knack for—or a desire to do—the business end of things. It was a real drag and things began to pile up, get lost, sit undone and create chaos," Eva confessed.

"It was fine when I was doing this all out of my dorm room, but when the business took off I was overwhelmed with the paperwork. Invoicing, purchase orders, bookkeeping, coordinating the shipping...it was maddening!"

Eva spent a couple of miserable months working 80-hour weeks and lamenting that she had started hating the very thing she loved most—making jewelry.

"I spent so little time actually making jewelry and finding unique gems to craft new pieces, that I actually considered hiring someone to make jewelry!"

But Eva came to her senses and hired someone to handle the essential but time-sucking jobs she hated. She hired Margie.

"What I realized from the get-go was that Margie was naturally a much better organizer than I was, and she was firmer and more decisive with vendors. She went through my piles of papers and within a week had all my bookkeeping, invoicing, and ordering up-to-date. I think she actually saved the business and even better, I now get to do what I really love—make jewelry," Eva beamed.

"Now that we're all sticking to our strengths, the business is better, and so am I."

Chapter 36. The First Hire of Many

Your VA is just the first hire you will make on the way to building your empire.

You will probably outgrow your off-site VA pretty quickly, or want to supplement her or him with a non-virtual, on-site, sitting-at-the-next-desk staff employee. No problem. I expect that kind of rapid growth from Growth Mavens. This is just the beginning of what your company will look like over the next year or two.

You will not stand still in one place for too long. The VA will give you that initial momentum. Think of it as an easy place to start. And that is the great part—you get to test the waters with your VA. And like the executive suites, this is a flexible solution. There are no long-term commitments or up-front costs. And if things don't work out as planned, you can easily take a step backward.

But as soon as your business warrants it, you will want to build a real team of on-site employees who are solely dedicated to the success of your company, unlike VAs who have other clients they must also attend to.

The building of a real organization is an absolutely critical step for Growth Mavens, and it is that desire that separates you from all other homebased entrepreneurs. It is also one of the main reasons why I had you move out of your home office and into a real office space. (Try to imagine for a moment where Microsoft, Dell, and Apple would be today if their founders stayed at home and never moved into a real office or hired any real employees.)

Chapter 37. Hiring Your First Employee: Your Assignments for Days 14–16

Day 14: Make a list of which time-sucking jobs you want to delegate, and how many hours you currently devote to these chores. Use the chart in the sidebar to help you organize your decisions.

Day 15: Find yourself a good virtual staffing agency on the Internet. There are some good ones out there and some not-so-good. And yes, I am affiliated with a virtual staffing agency (big surprise) through my web site, GetAVirtualAssistant.com, and I definitely believe we are one of the good ones. But whether you choose to use us or someone else, know that a good staffing agency will work hard to get you connected to the right VA for your business. You'll be assigned a competent project manager who, after understanding your requirements, will do all the vetting and heavy lifting to find the perfect VA for you. Anything less than that should make you move on.

Day 16: Contact the virtual staffing agency and ask to speak with a project manager to discuss your specific needs and goals. Schedule a telephone conversation with your new VA and, using the list you made on Day 14, determine which time-sucking jobs you should give to her (or him). When you speak with her, compare thoughts about how much time each task will take. If your estimate is wildly different from your VA's, ask to speak to the project manager again. If you're on the same page—set up a work schedule and start handing off your time-sucking jobs.

The Chart

Take a look at this nifty organizational chart—it can help you see the jobs you have, and who will complete them. I based this on a similar concept that you've probably already read about in The E-Myth Revisited by Michael E. Gerber. Right now your name will be in most of the boxes, but the idea is to outsource as much of the work as possible to other people. Your goal should be to get your name out of most of the boxes—except for the growth-creating, revenue-producing ones—and get someone else's name in them.

I've used my friend Harry Bell—a great entrepreneur and an avid outsourcer of jobs—and his information-products company as an example of how the chart can work. Notice that he doesn't have a staff of executives, because he is happy to fill that role in this stage of his company's development.

This is high-level work he is willing to do, so the top boxes are almost all Harry. But notice the middle and bottom boxes—they are all outsourced to other people.

This is a good example of how to create growth in your company.

continued

See? There isn't much of Harry anywhere on the bottom of this chart. He is doing the big work. The Growth Maven work. He lets the crew do the rest.

Now, you do it. Create a similar organizational chart (on scrap paper—don't make this a big exercise) and put your name in all the boxes for the jobs that you do every day. You probably will be in almost every box.

Now start thinking about replacing yourself. Start with the lowest-level jobs first—most likely those that are secretarial and administrative. Each time you take your name out of a box and add someone else's, you have more time to do revenue-producing work. This is how you are going to grow your business—one employee at a time, one less time-sucking job (for you) at a time.

Growth Maven Organizational Chart

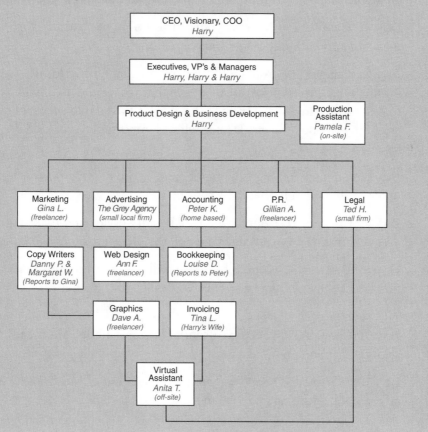

The Wrap Up: Days 1–16

Don't move to the next section until you have worked each of these assignments, one every day. Here they are again:

Day 1: (Chapter 10) Be clear that you have a Home Office From Hell and are ready to change your business. Then, take the quiz and discover who you are—a Lifestyle Guru or a Growth Maven.

Day 2: (Chapter 29) Figure out how to find all of the available executive suites and shared office space located in your geographic area of interest.

Day 3: (Chapter 29) Once you've completed your search and narrowed your list of executive suites and/or shared office spaces in your preferred locations, start calling them to find out what spaces are available, their asking prices, what's included in the rent, if there are any additional charges, and so on.

Day 4: (Chapter 29) Narrow your list to no more than five top choices and make an appointment to tour each location.

Day 5: (Chapter 29) You should be able to visit all five locations in one day. Conduct the same type of due diligence that you would use if you were looking to rent an apartment. Go back to the checklists and make a list of questions to ask, things to look for, etc. Decide what is important to you and do not deviate from your plan.

Day 6: (Chapter 29) Sign the agreement and pay any up-front fees (security deposit, etc.). Plan to make the move.

Day 7: (Chapter 31) Contact the U.S. Postal Service and make a business address change. Get boxes. Make sure all the office paperwork is in order.

Day 8: (Chapter 31) Decide how you will conduct the move. Make arrangements with people who will help you move and decide how you will repay them.

Day 9: (Chapter 31) Pack nonessential business items. Mark each box with a clear description and make a list of supplies you will need for the new office.

Day 10: (Chapter 31) Send out an announcement of your move. Get together all the phone numbers you will need for the move day.

DAYS 1–16

WRAP-UP

Day 11: (Chapter 31) Shop for new supplies and pack more nonessential business items. Check with office manager to confirm move-in time and any last-minute instructions. Confirm that the phone and Internet have been turned on.

Day 12: (Chapter 31) Do the last business that needs to be done. Pack all the essential business items into a "Top Priority" box. Call helpers and have them meet at a single place at a specific time and let them know the plan. Get a handful of petty cash for tips.

WRAP-UP

Day 13: (Chapter 31) Moving Day! Give everyone a task and set them to work. Set up the staging area while boxes are being moved in.

Day 14: (Chapter 37) Make a list of which time-sucking jobs you want to delegate and how many hours you currently devote to these chores. Use the chart to help you organize your decisions.

Day 15: (Chapter 37) Find yourself a good virtual staffing agency.

Day 16: (Chapter 37) Contact the virtual staffing agency and discuss your specific needs. Set up a schedule with your new VA. Prepare to get rid of time-sucking jobs.

Part 4

I Want a Business That Supports My Great Life!

A Primer for Lifestyle Gurus

"You know you are on the road to success if you would do your job, and not be paid for it."

—Oprah Winfrey

Chapter 38. I Want to Make a Great Living . . . In My Underwear

Many entrepreneurs do not live to work. They work to live and they want a business that will help them have more free time, flexible hours, weekends off without a single client phone call. They want to make a nice, comfortable income while they are living their lives.

The good news is you can make this happen. You Lifestyle Gurus can pull in a perfectly respectable low to mid six-figure income and still have time to do many of the things you've always wanted to do—pick the kids up from school every day, work four days a week, have every weekend free, and be with your family at 5 P.M.

Whatever your dream of the perfect business, you can make it happen because Lifestyle Gurus have the secret. You know that your business is supposed to work for you so that you don't have to postpone all the fun until your retirement 30 years from now—if you ever get one. You know that the fun starts today and you need a business that will keep the bills paid, give you plenty of freedom money (money to support your hobbies and leisure activities), and give you more time to spend with the people you love. And don't forget the work. You do want to love your work—you just want interesting and challenging work from the best-paying clients.

No problem. You've got 100 days to make it happen!

Chapter 39. It's What They See That Counts

I'd bet that most people are a little envious of Lifestyle Gurus.

Yes, even those ambitious Growth Mavens who are out there chomping at the bit to crush the industry giants with their next brilliant idea. I think everyone at one time or another wishes they could, just once in awhile, kick back and not worry about a client over the long weekend or play a little hooky and go sport fishing on a Wednesday. Many of us entrepreneurs wish we could throw the ball around with our kids at 4 P.M., but most of us don't.

Why? Because we're the boss.

If you're anything like me, I'm pretty sure that when you first started your company you thought being the boss meant that you could do what you wanted, when you wanted—right? And I'm also pretty sure that it didn't take you long to figure out that being the boss really meant handling every little crisis, managing last-minute client requests, urgent cash-flow issues, and heaps of invoices and paperwork. The list is endless.

So, Lifestyle Gurus need to find ways to make sure their lives come first and their businesses follow along.

They want to be in their bathrobes working at the keyboard without appearing to be. They need to make their companies appear big even when they are quite small.

They need to be polished in their appearance so that clients see them as viable contenders in the marketplace. They need to appear powerful and competent, not disorganized and scattered.

Clients, particularly great-paying clients, want to give their business to entrepreneurs who inspire trust. They avoid fly-by-night operators in favor of those companies that look like they will be around for years to come.

These clients are looking for companies that can deliver stellar work on deadline. Until they get to know you and the quality of your work, potential clients can only judge you by *what they see*.

They will hire your competition every time if your infant is screaming in the background during conference calls, or if they have to sit on lawn chairs in your bedroom to hear your proposal.

They want your complete focus. They want you to have an impeccable presentation. They are noticing your office, how you dress, how confident you look, how tight your talk is, how organized you seem.

And no matter how you stack it, meeting in your living room or in a local Starbucks does not exactly scream out that your company is best of breed.

I can help you stay in your pajamas and still make an impressive impression.

Entrepreneur Story: Judith Addison

 "I couldn't be happier to have left my cubicle," Judith Addison told me at a recent cocktail party.

She left the entertainment marketing firm where she had worked for some eight years.

"By the time I opened my own small firm, I had soaked up every bit of knowledge I could from my employer. I worked with big accounts, little accounts, crazy narcissists, and some of the best and brightest. I felt like I had done it all, and I went into my new business with a certain degree of confidence that I would continue that success."

And Judith wasn't wrong. Her small consulting firm started to grow like crazy. Her reputation for getting the details right, a commitment to hands-on customer service, and her huge Rolodex of contacts attracted some big brands to her company.

"We were turning great potential clients away. I was so happy I made this decision. But I was working from seven in the morning until midnight. It was worse than when I was sitting in a cubicle."

Judith wanted her dream business, but she also wanted a life. She had survived breast cancer just three years before. She and her husband dreamed of flying his plane to Brazil with their two teenage sons. They planned on living abroad for three months out of every year. She wanted to work four days a week, not seven.

"I'm not an empire builder. What I am is a woman who wants to have a lot of adventures in the second half of my life. I want to know that my business will be there when I get back from a safari in Africa or a long weekend with my sons at the beach."

Judith is not alone.

Chapter 40. Why Can't I Meet My Clients at Home or at Starbucks? There's Nothing Wrong with That, Right?

Business publications are often filled with excellent advice for homebased businesses. However I recently came upon several columns from different publications urging homebased entrepreneurs to find creative places to have business meetings with their clients.

"I can't meet in my living room because it's a dark cave of papers and office supplies," says John Nash from Tacoma, Washington, "so we have to meet in a public space."

John's meeting room of choice is a diner down the street from his home. He and his clients talk business over stale coffee and grilled cheese sandwiches.

"It's not the best scenario, but it's cheap and my clients don't seem to mind."

In fact, many professionals agree with John and say that small businesspeople should take advantage of cheap public spaces to handle client meetings. They say it doesn't impact their credibility, image, or reputation.

I completely disagree. This is extremely poor advice for entrepreneurs who are trying to get their businesses off the ground because—to use a cliché—first impressions count.

Who you are, the way you speak, the way you dress, the way your work looks, how you manage your finances and cash flow, the environment where you work, where you meet your clients—it all matters. Every little detail sends a message about who you are and what you believe. Every detail helps a prospective client make the decision to say "yes" or "no," especially if there is a lot of money on the line or if your client has to justify his decision to his bosses.

That means that every interaction counts. And meeting in a diner over a day-old Danish isn't going to cut it if you want to grow your business, get better clients, and make more money.

How to Have Your Cake and Eat It, Too!

Face it. It matters where you do your business.

You can work at home and still have professional digs for meetings and presentations. You can make a splash without having to move into some formal cubicle environment that you were trying to run from in the first place.

You can still be a renegade and make your clients fall in love with you. You are classier than a cheeseburger at the local diner and not nearly as conformist as a grande mocha frappuccino at the Java Bean.

You can stay at home and still have alternatives!

Chapter 41. The Five Places You Should Never, *Ever* Meet with a Client

All of these places have been recommended as potential meeting sites by professional consultants. Frankly, I think it's horrible advice.

1. Starbucks or any other wi-fi–equipped coffee house

Starbucks has really become the king of the cheap public meeting places, and a spate of similarly equipped coffee houses have cropped up on almost every block. I've read that the plush chairs, "eclectic snack food," and infinite supply of java are the big selling points.

Fine. But you do not want to meet your clients at tiny, coffee-stained tables, surrounded by students and a bunch of aspiring 20-year-old novelists. No, you want to be able to have an adult conversation and make strong points without worrying about bothering the folks at the table six inches from you. Starbucks is serviceable and cheap, but it is not an environment that will help you make an impression that inspires trust, confidence, and loyalty.

2. Barnes and Noble, Borders, or any other high-end bookstore

Some consultants believe that bookstores offer a quiet, intellectual feel when meeting with clients. This is ridiculous! They think this, of course, only because the place has a lot of books. Books or no books, meeting in Borders does not send the message that you are smart, together, knowledgeable, and savvy.

College students and down-on-their-luck artists meet in bookstores. You must create an image of success, even if you are still a struggling startup. People want to invest in and work with winners. If you do not take your own business seriously, no one else will, either.

3. Public libraries

Not sexy but definitely quiet. According to some of my colleagues, libraries offer a place to meet all day and no one will make you buy anything. I've been informed that some libraries even offer conference rooms you can use.

No matter how practical, the message that you send is that you have no resources. You are basically telling your clients that the best you can do is muster up an ill-equipped room in a public library. There is little opportunity for you to make a huge impression, and most likely the technology, such as videoconferencing and presentation platforms, will not be state-of-the-art or reliable. You cannot afford to leave your image up to chance!

4. Hotel lobbies

Hotel lobbies can be beautiful and on the outside might seem like a great space to meet. But they are also extremely busy. There is a lot of foot traffic, including large groups of tourists and a few children's choirs passing through. Hotel guests on vacation do not care if you make a good impression with your client. The hotel employees will not cater to your needs unless you are a guest.

You cannot control your environment here. You cannot create a look of professionalism. You may end up shouting your well-prepared points over a group of drunken salespeople. Give your business and your ideas a platform that you can control. The fewer people around, the more ability you have to make a lasting, positive impression.

5. McDonald's or any fast-food restaurant

One consultant recently informed his readership that McDonald's had started offering free wi-fi in some of its urban franchises.

He said this like it was a good thing!

Just because your local McDonald's offers free wi-fi and discount chocolate sundaes does not mean you should meet a client there anytime soon.

I love the occasional chocolate glazed donut from Dunkin' Donuts and have enjoyed a Big Mc or two over the years, but that is not something you should share with a client, especially a client whose business you are trying to win.

You are trying to sell yourself as high-end, something special, a cut above the competition. When your client thinks of you, you do not want him to say, "That Joe, we always meet at Arby's." You want him to say, "That Joe does some outstanding work for our firm—what a pro!"

These little things stay with people, so make sure that everything you do represents you well.

Chapter 42. Virtual Office Space: Stay at Home and Your Clients Will Never Know . . . Unless You Tell Them

So what are these alternatives?

I almost always recommend that my homebased clients get a virtual office space. This way they can work from home while giving the appearance that their businesses are much larger and more impressive. This is absolutely essential if you want to attract and catch the bigger fish.

Here's how it works: For a reasonable monthly fee, you can rent the services of an office suite without actually renting the office itself. Sounds crazy, right? Imagine working from your suburban house outside New York City, but coming into Manhattan and having your client meetings in a fully equipped, state-of-the-art conference room in a luxury office building.

That means you can finish up the big client presentation at home and go to your very own conference room in a high-end office suite. Your clients can sip a cup of freshly brewed coffee while you knock 'em dead with your professionalism.

Two weeks later your super-impressed clients sign the deal. Not bad for a conference room that only costs you a few dollars each month and is available to you on an "as needed" basis.

Stay at home, but get all the advantages of being in a "real" office. Say *sayonara* to Starbucks and a less-than-impressive reputation!

Entrepreneur Story: Barbara Young

 Barbara Young owns a small consulting business in Atlanta, Georgia. The keyword here is "small" because Barbara knows that her competition has more money, a bigger reputation, and more marketing resources.

"What I had going for me was personal service and attention to the client, but I was working out of my spare bedroom and calling it an office," said Barbara.

"I needed to keep my overhead low, so I had no intention of leaving my home office. But I also needed to pull off a polished, professional appearance when I met with potential clients. In a nutshell, I needed to make my business look bigger than it really was."

In Barbara's case, she didn't need a receptionist to answer the phone since part of her business' strength was that her clients could always reach her directly. She didn't want to compromise a core value, but she did need to have an office space or conference room where she could do her presentations using state-of-the-art technology, where her clients could work at a spacious conference table, and where she could wow them with her creativity.

At my suggestion, Barbara rented a conference room in a nearby executive suite for ten hours each month. "Most of my clients just assume the suite is my fulltime office. Other longtime clients know that I work from home," said Barbara, "but they respect how I have crafted a professional, flexible environment that allows us to get the best work done."

Barbara chose ten hours of conference room time, but you can choose as much or as little as you need. The important thing to remember is that even if you are operating your business from your home, you still need to run it as a first-class operation.

As Barbara told me, "My clients love that I am savvy enough to care about the details. That already tells them something important about me and my work."

Chapter 43. It's a Bit Like an A La Carte Menu

A virtual office lets you stay at home in, say, Queens (New York) and have a prestigious Manhattan address and phone number. That's what I have. Call my Manhattan number and you're likely to have me pick up in my slippers in Queens. My calls are automatically routed to my home office phone. You can do that or you can have your calls routed anywhere you want: your cell phone, vacation house, or hotel room.

You can rent a prestigious Fifth Avenue address for your business and never leave your bedroom or get out of your pajamas. The office suite can collect your mail and forward it to your home. If you choose, a professional receptionist can answer your calls with your company name and take messages per your instructions.

It's like ordering just the good stuff off the menu—you get to choose which services are best for your business and you only pay for what you need. So you keep your costs down while making your operation appear bigger and stronger.

Chapter 44. Eight Ways Virtual Office Space Can Make You Look Big—Even When You're Not

1. Have a professional receptionist answer your calls using your company's name and/or set up personalized voicemail messages.
2. Get a prestigious business address that you can use on business cards, letterhead, and marketing materials.
3. Get a local phone number with a desirable area code, and have your calls forwarded right to your bedroom office or anywhere else.
4. Have your mail, packages, and messenger deliveries collected and forwarded to your home office.
5. Use conference and meeting rooms as much or as little as needed and be able to change your level of services on demand.

6. Have your company name listed in the lobby of the building even though you don't technically have an office there.

7. Have a network of branch offices by getting a virtual office space in key cities.

8. Prevent clients from dropping by your house at odd hours when you are unprepared.

Chapter 45. Getting Your Virtual Office Space: Your Assignments for Days 2–7

Let's get you a virtual office.

The first thing you need to do is find virtual office (VO) space in your geographic area. The VOs are a service that is almost always offered by an executive suite company. (I discuss executive suites in detail in Chapter 17 in the Growth Maven section of this book.) You'll need to find all the executive suites located in your geographic area of interest. You can attack this a couple of different ways:

VO Search #1...
Day 2: Look through the Yellow Pages, do an online search, scan the classified real estate sections of your local newspapers, and scroll through the listings on Craigslist.

Day 3: Once you've completed your search and narrowed down your list of executive suites in your preferred locations, start calling them to find out what virtual office space packages they offer and what their prices are.

Day 4: Narrow down your list to no more than your five top choices and make an appointment to tour each location.

Day 5: You should be able to visit all five locations in one day.

Day 6: Sign the agreement and pay any up-front fees (security deposit, etc.).

Day 7: Start using your new VO!

Or VO Search #2

Day 2: You can go to GetAVirtualOffice.com where you'll see pictures, addresses, and a full description of the facility, and then you'll be able to sign up directly online with a credit card. No need to call the different centers or to visit them all. If you have any questions, you can call a toll-free help line. The whole thing should take you less than 30 or 60 minutes—all in one day!

Yes, I own GetAVirtualOffice.com, so if you use this website, you'll be putting a few bucks into my pocket (paid for by the executive suite owner, not by you). My wife will thank you and when my daughter calls from college asking for more money, I will silently be thanking you, as well. But feel no pressure to use us. Check us out and if you think we are the best option for you, great. If not, go with someone else—but one way or another you must get yourself a virtual office space today!

Days 3–7: You're done! This method buys you five extra days to make more money, develop something new for your business, get to the beach, or just kick back with a glass of wine and enjoy a little extra free time.

Chapter 46. You Are Sitting at Home but Your Clients Think You Have an Office on Fifth Avenue—Now What?

So you are at home, still basking in the coolness of being able to make a big impression even while you stay small. You can now wow your clients by appearing more professional, more together, and more polished than your competitors.

But wait! Nothing has really changed, has it?

You have a new place to conduct meetings and meet clients, but your business is still basically the same. Sure, you look more polished and professional. But is that new conference room really going to provide the major overhaul you were looking for?

Probably not.

You are still mowed under by piles of papers that haven't been filed, bills that haven't been paid, and invoices that haven't been processed or mailed in weeks. And speaking of mowing, you could feed cows on that lawn of yours. Better schedule a little yard work in between the invoices and emptying the waste basket of all those crumpled bits of paper you threw in there trying to come up with the perfect tag line for your client's new campaign.

Oops! Just stepped over your estimated taxes on the floor. Guess you should've mailed those out—last month. And you won't have time to get started on marketing your business to the Chamber of Commerce, so cross that off the list and try to fit it in sometime next week.

The jobs are endless—and your new conference room won't solve that.

You'll have to hire staff.

Chapter 47. Staff? I Started This Business so I Didn't Have to Deal with Staff

Maybe so, but I think you are starting to realize that you can't possibly do everything yourself.

Now don't start freaking out and thinking you'll have nine Harvard graduates milling around your basement office while you are banging away at your laptop in your pajamas. I mean you need to delegate the drudgework—the time-sucking, business-killing drudgework—that keeps you from having the time to create a better, stronger business.

Think of it this way—how much is your time worth per hour? What do you charge your clients? One hundred dollars per hour? Two hundred? Three hundred? More? Whatever you charge, imagine paying someone that amount per hour to file your papers and send out your invoices. Would you really pay someone $200 per hour for that work?

Of course not, but you just did!

Think about what you did today. How much of it was drudgework? How much time did you spend paying bills and doing other administrative tasks? Wouldn't that time have been better spent trying to market your business, or finding a new joint venture partner?

That is $200-per-hour work. See what I mean? You can't afford to keep paying yourself $200 an hour to do menial chores. It will kill your business.

What you need is to outsource the time-sucking administrative jobs and focus on what is important; maintaining and enhancing your business (so you can take a lot of long weekends and vacations in places without cell phone coverage or e-mail).

Chapter 48. What Did You Do at Work Today?

Your job is to create a great company that can run on autopilot even if you are on the slopes or coaching your kid's soccer game. You cannot be on the sidelines screaming into the phone about purchase orders and distribution. You need someone who can do the screaming for you.

Why?

Because a real Lifestyle Guru knows that having a life means not micromanaging and controlling the whole show. Lifestyle Gurus value quality time and they know that by trying to do everything—especially the drudgework—they will end up with less time and more work than when they were back in the cubicle.

Anything less will kill your leisure time, keep you away from the things you really love, and lower your income.

You need to decide which of your daily jobs are revenue-producing, and which are non-revenue-producing time-suckers. Revenue-producing jobs are those that help you build the business—meeting clients, developing new strategies to market your business, positioning yourself as an expert in front of your customer base, etc. This is the stuff that only you should do, because you do it best.

Time-sucking tasks are the ones better suited to other people. They include:

1. Professional jobs requiring specific skill sets, such as accounting, advertising, bookkeeping, legal, website design, etc., and
2. Administrative jobs, such as setting appointments, data entry, filing, invoicing, order processing, etc.

Lifestyle Gurus cannot afford to do time-sucking jobs.

I want you to decide right now—which critical revenue-producing tasks you and only you should be doing, and which non-revenue-producing, time-sucking tasks you can delegate to a competent professional.

Chapter 49. Lone Wolf—It's Me Against the World!

I have to admit that turning over control to someone else can be terrifying.

This is a big problem for most Lifestyle Gurus. If you want to remain that free-flying, wings-unclipped maverick you imagined in your daydreams while you were back in the cubicle, you'll need to unburden yourself from the tedious, time-sucking tasks that are bogging you down. You don't want to become that stodgy old boss you left behind, and you certainly don't want to end up as an administrator, managing people and dealing with their issues for several hours out of every day.

I imagine that many of you Lifestyle Gurus think it might be easier to just stay the lone wolf. And I agree it is tempting. But you must resist it. The home office cave can seem like a very comfortable place to go to everyday, but you can get stuck there and become increasingly isolated from the rest of the world. Sooner or later, your business will suffer, as well.

When that happens, your lifestyle—the time with friends, kids, spouses—gets smaller and smaller until you are killing yourself 24/7 and wondering how it all happened.

Outsourcing is crucial. That's why I want you to outsource at least one area of drudgework to someone else. Pick jobs you hate and are bad at. Pick jobs that could be done better by someone who doesn't hate doing it.

Real Lifestyle Gurus know that they cannot work in a box all by themselves. They need to delegate almost everything except for the high-level jobs that only they can do. That's how they make lots of money and have plenty of leisure time.

Chapter 50. I Like Being Chief Cook and Bottle Washer

Maybe. But you might be a better chief than a bottle washer.

Are you bad at keeping the books? Always messing up your taxes? Think you have to be the size of IBM to have a bookkeeper? Wrong. If you hate doing the books, you've probably been putting it off and accruing late charges and penalties on your unpaid bills. And because you hate it, you're probably also screwing it up, which means that it will end up costing you even more money when your accountant tries to sort everything out at tax time.

Because you hate it, you don't invest any time in learning about innovations in that area, so you don't know the latest tricks and short cuts. More money down the drain.

Think you might be too small for a bookkeeper? Wrong. A client of mine runs a small marketing consulting company. He told me that he held off getting a book-keeper for the longest time because he was afraid a real professional would not take his small business financials seriously.

"What I realized is that we had a lot of accounting activity, like billing and in-voices, even though we were not swimming in money."

In the end, not only did my client's bookkeeper save him nearly $20,000 that first year, but my client used those freed-up hours to focus on a new marketing strategy that's now bringing in almost $5,000 in new business every month.

You aren't saving money doing everything yourself—you're losing money!

Chapter 51. The Top Seven Outsources for Homebased Businesses

1. Bookkeeping and accounting

Unload the paperwork and save time, money, and frustration. Bookkeepers and ac-countants can keep your accounts, manage your receivables and payables, and deal with tax issues. The tax laws are constantly changing and the government is unfor-giving if you don't pay or underpay your taxes.

2. Legal services

Unless you're an attorney, don't even attempt to do this stuff yourself. That can be one of the quickest ways to end up in court and out of business.

3. Virtual assistants (VAs)

VAs are a godsend for Lifestyle Gurus because they provide a low-commitment, low-cost solution that can free you up to do the important revenue-producing jobs and still leave you with plenty of time to enjoy life.

Not only that, VAs are small business owners themselves, so they completely un-derstand the entrepreneurial mindset. You want someone who can empathize with your daily challenges, and knows firsthand the importance of providing great cus-tomer service.

VAs work off-site (typically from their own home offices), so you don't have to pay for employee benefits, payroll taxes, office supplies, vacations, etc. They provide their own supplies and equipment. You pay them hourly and they only work the hours you need them. That means if you have two hours of telephone calls to return, data entry, and creating sales reports, you only pay for those two hours.

The VAs are pros, and many of them have specialized skills, such as bookkeeping, web design, and writing. And if you use a virtual staffing agency (similar to a temp agency), you'll be assigned a project manager who will work with you to find the right VA or combination of VAs to get your various jobs done.

With a virtual staffing agency there's no need to review résumés, interview candidates, etc.—your project manager will handle all of that for you. And if you don't love your VA you can always trade one in for another.

There are no pesky personal problems or issues, just a clear mandate to rid yourself of work that is a drain on your time and ability to live your life.

4. Public relations

You won't need a top-of-the-line PR firm at your disposal, but getting freelancers to help write a press release for the launch of your new product or to help you get some coverage in the hometown newspaper is a good use of their time and your money.

5. Advertising and marketing

You don't need an entire agency, just a competent professional who can help you create a plan for getting the word out about your business. A competent ad person can figure out whom you should be talking to and the best ways to get their attention.

6. Writing and ghostwriting

Want to write a killer press release? A great speech for the local Chamber of Commerce? Want to author an article for your local paper? These are great ways to get media attention for your business, except they are time-sucking jobs and are often best left to the professionals. Freelance writers can be hired on a project-by-project basis at a reasonable cost to make you look good without all the time-sucking work.

7. Other specialized services

These are the jobs that can only—and should only—be done by skilled professionals. These include: graphic design, website programming, etc.

Outsourcing? Nine Things to Do

Follow these tips from entrepreneurs who have outsourced and lived to tell the tale:

1. *Carefully evaluate what jobs are critical (revenue producing) and best handled by you, and what should go to someone else. You should do the jobs that move your business forward and leave the drudgework for the freelancer.*

2. *Be specific about what you need from the freelancer. The more specific you are and the more details you can give them about what you expect, the better the result will be.*

3. *Do your due diligence up front. It's hard to know if people will provide a good fit by speaking to them a couple of times, but find out as much as you can about them and their work before you bring them on. The more information you have, the better the outcome will be for everyone. Get references and copies of their previous work if possible.*

4. *Start slowly. You don't have to give away the farm right away. Start freelancers off with a small project to see how they do. Then ramp up to larger, more high-paying jobs.*

5. *Be upfront about pay and what they can expect. If you say you will be able to pay them more in three months, make sure you do it.*

6. *Want to make your freelancer happy? Always pay on time. Freelancers often have to chase down money from their clients. You will be at the top of their list of important work if you pay on time.*

7. *Let the freelancer know you are a small, homebased business. You have different needs than a large company with systems in place. Your freelancer needs to be comfortable working in a more relaxed, less formal environment.*

8. *Know how you define success. What will be the best-case scenario for you? Know what you want to happen, then make all your interactions work toward that goal.*

9. *Make sure you have freelancers and virtual assistants sign both a Non-Disclosure Agreement (NDA)—this ensures that all your information remains confidential—and a Work-For-Hire Agreement—this ensures that the work they do for you and any of their creations, designs, etc., belong to you and not to them.*

Chapter 52. Virtual Assistants Are a Lifestyle Guru's Best Friends

Want to leave work early and head out to the beach for a long weekend? How about taking off for a few days and sleeping in a tent in the mountains? Maybe you want to be a chaperone for your kid's class on a school trip? Whatever fun thing you Lifestyle Gurus want to do, a VA can help you do it.

VAs provide a great opportunity to delegate your non-revenue-producing tasks. They are low commitment and low cost, so if you don't like working with them you haven't lost much. One of the best scenarios for Lifestyle Gurus is having someone who is more than happy to do your dirty work but isn't working side by side with you at your kitchen table.

They are doing work that you would normally have to do yourself, but instead, you are out enjoying life. How about that?

Chapter 53. What Can a VA Do for a Lifestyle Guru?

In a phrase—give you more time.

Start making a list of time-sucking, energy-robbing jobs that you can't wait to hand off to your VA starting tomorrow. If you're having trouble, this list should get you started:

- Creating and maintaining your mailing list
- Responding to customer calls and e-mails
- Responding to comments on your blog
- Putting together your weekly/monthly schedules
- Scheduling and coordinating meetings, appointments (professional and personal), and interviews
- Researching business trips, vacations, and travel destinations
- Booking hotels and flights
- Researching competitors, potential partners, vendors, and clients on the Internet

- Bookkeeping and light accounting, including paying bills, data entry into Quick-Books, expense reports, etc.
- Making changes to your blog or website and working with your web person
- Managing shipping and distribution of your products
- Arranging speaking opportunities (read the rest of the book and you'll know why this is important!)
- Sending articles and columns off to various magazine editors (read on for this one, too!)
- Designing presentations

Chapter 54. As with Everything, There Are The Usual Drawbacks

VAs are not perfect. Here are a couple of things to keep in mind when you get one:

- VAs typically cost $30 or more per hour (depending on where they're based and if you require specialized skills). Sounds astronomical but you will have no outside expenses (taxes and benefits) and you are only paying for the hours they work, so your VA will not be costing you while they're out having lunch, on vacation, or out sick.
- VAs are not well-suited for last-minute projects. You should be able to think about what needs to be done on a consistent ongoing basis, and create a set list of projects for them to complete. You shouldn't throw last-minute tasks at VAs. Since VAs have other clients besides you, they may not be able to accommodate last-minute or urgent requests; if they are able, it might be at a premium rate.
- You have to be organized to use VAs effectively. They are best used for specific and ongoing tasks. "Research snowboarding in the Alps." "Create a flow chart." "Update the invoices." They work best with concrete and specific tasks, so get clear about what you want and make the instructions clear.
- It is possible to get a bum VA, but if you use a virtual staffing agency you can simply speak to your project manager and have a new one assigned to you.
- Lifestyle Gurus are often a little like lone wolves—they like to go it alone. They sometimes find managing other people to be challenging. Even though they are

off site, you still have to manage your VAs, give them clear-cut expectations and a clear mandate for the tasks you want completed, and provide them with a foundation to get the job done for you. This is not always an easy skin to slip into for the Lifestyle Guru, but you'll have to do it to get the most value out of your VA.

Using a VA will help you learn to delegate and create clear instructions. Also, remember to think about what your expectations are for your VA. When you speak to the project manager make sure you tell them what kind of person you are looking for—the qualities and skills that are important to you.

You want to set this up for success right from the get-go.

Chapter 55. From the Mouths of VAs . . .

I asked three VAs with over 40 years of experience between them to talk about what worked best with their clients. Here's what they had to say:

Give your VA the time and resources to get acquainted with your business.

VAs are not mind readers and they cannot know exactly what you want or how you want it done unless you tell them. Invest in them and help them get to know the job by sending them materials about your business and correct examples of work. Spend some time talking to them about your business and what you are trying to achieve. Let them know what worked and what didn't work for you in the past.

"I do a lot better with clients who take the time to send me information, get me to websites, and teach me about their businesses," said Ann, a VA from Seattle who specializes in marketing and business writing.

"I can really dive in and get a lot done for them because I now know what they are trying to achieve."

Don't be afraid to tell them your weaknesses, as well as strengths. If you have a tendency to be cryptic when explaining things, there is no harm in saying, "I can be a little vague sometimes, so if you don't get what I'm saying, ask me to clarify."

Get an estimate from your VA on how much time they will need to complete the project.

That way, there will be no surprise costs or unmet expectations. People like to know the rules. It makes them feel comfortable. Ask the VA to look at the workload and estimate the time needed to accomplish it. Is that acceptable to you? Of course you want it done as quickly as possible, but find out what reasonable time the VA needs to do it.

"I like it when clients are clear with me about how much time they want me to spend on a project and what their budget is," said Rosie, a VA with 15 years of experience working directly for CEOs.

"In return, I let them know how I am progressing and whether the job is taking more or less time than we expected. That means everyone knows what is happening and there is less anxiety."

Your VA has office hours and other clients.

You cannot pummel your VA with last-minute work or add extra hours at the last minute. More importantly, you must respect their schedule. They do not work into the wee hours of the night and they don't want you to check in on the project at 10 P.M.

"I had a client who always gave me five hours of work and expected me to do it in two," said Ann. "Then he called me all evening and hounded me until it was done. Needless to say, that relationship didn't work because his demands impacted my personal life, my other clients, and my ability to get their work done. I ended the relationship."

If you don't want your VA calling you at 2 A.M., you shouldn't be calling them at that time, either.

VAs are virtual and they will not be coming into your office to work.

Some people are happy with the off-site work relationship until a big project comes in and they want the VA to work on-site. That might be better for you but it is not better for the VA.

"I have an office full of equipment and no real desire to work in someone else's office," said Melanie, a mother of two young sons.

"I have a homebased business, too, and I have one for a reason."

VAs will not be working in your office, so don't try to convince them. They are entrepreneurs and fellow Lifestyle Gurus. Let them stay where they are and do their job.

Give your VA a list of jobs and priorities at the beginning of each week, and include a time expectation.

"My best clients are the ones who are specific about what they need to have done," said Rosie.

"I like to know exactly what needs to be done for the week, when they want the project completed, and how many hours they think it will take. This way I know we are on the same page, and I have it in writing."

When you put something in writing, it makes you accountable. Give your VAs a written list of jobs. They'll know what you expect, and you'll know what they are working on. Everyone is accountable and on the same page.

Entrepreneur Story: Mitch Parado

"I was sinking."

Mitch Parado could chuckle about it now. He even cracked a joke or two. But when he started his small technology business, he never dreamed he would be working from six in the morning to midnight.

"I started this business because I'm a single dad and I wanted to spend more time with my daughter," Mitch said.

"Instead, I was on my Blackberry during dinner and taking phone calls at her middle school. It was pathetic. I was a slave. All I did was work and still it was not enough."

Then he confessed.

"My daughter wanted to get my attention and she couldn't, so she sent me an instant message. Wow! What a wake-up call that this wasn't working!"

Mitch made a big error. He did everything himself. He was used to it. He was raising his daughter on his own. He was competent, capable, and smart. So why not, right? He had always done everything on his own, and he did it better than most. Mitch had the mindset that many people have. It begins with, "If you want something done right..."

You know the rest.

The last straw came when he realized he had never billed for a large job that

continued

he had done a few months before.

"I worked so hard for this major client for months, and I was so overworked that I forgot to bill them for the work I had done," he said chuckling, realizing how crazy that was.

"This and the IM from my kid made me realize that I missed the whole point of being on my own."

The answer for Mitch was a VA.

"I'm great with computers but I'm a bit of an administrative mess," Mitch confesses.

"Angela, my VA, has some light bookkeeping experience and a great organizational head, and we set out a plan for working together."

Angela works about six hours a week for Mitch, and they've gotten into a routine. Mitch says she knows the business so well now she barely needs any instruction. She lets him know what needs to be done and does it.

When I spoke with Angela she said she loved their working relationship.

"We have a groove. I know what he needs and we just check in and make sure we are on the same page. Then he leaves me alone while I get the work done," she said.

"I like that he doesn't over-manage me."

And Mitch likes that he now gets paid on time for his completed projects.

Chapter 56. Hiring a VA: Your Assignments for Days 8–13

Day 8: Make a general list of which time-sucking jobs you may want to delegate and how many hours you currently devote to these chores. You won't have the complete list together at this point, but you'll need to have an outline in mind so you can give the virtual staffing agency an idea of the kind of person who might work for you. We'll develop this list more in the coming days.

Day 9: Find yourself a good virtual staffing agency on the Internet.

Day 10: Contact the virtual staffing agency and discuss your specific needs and goals.

Day 11: Finalize paperwork with the agency. Phone your new VA and say, "Hi."

Day 12: Create a list of time-sucking jobs you will give to your VA with specific instructions to follow and your time expectations for each task. Send it to your new VA and follow up with a phone call. Set up a work schedule with your new VA.

Day 13: Get on to more important revenue-generating work.

The Chart

I have a handy organizational chart for Lifestyle Gurus. This chart, like the one in the Growth Maven section, was inspired by The E-Myth Revisited by Michael E. Gerber. I jiggered a few things around to help you see what jobs you should be doing and what jobs you should be outsourcing.

Right now your name will be in most if not all of the boxes, but the idea is to outsource as much of the grunt work as possible to other people. Your goal should be to get your name out of the boxes that are not revenue-generating and put someone else's name in. That's how you get weekends off, more vacations, and quality time with your kids.

I've used my friend Helen Rubens—an extremely successful Lifestyle Guru—as an example of how the chart can work. Helen's company makes hand-painted and carved signs, and she sells them all over the world to upscale clients. Each one is made with painstaking attention to detail, so they make very few but sell them at top dollar.

Notice that Helen, as an artist, is involved in the design and production of the signs and has outsourced the administrative work. This decision has made the business very fulfilling for her since she gets to do what she loves—the actual designing and crafting of the signs.

continued

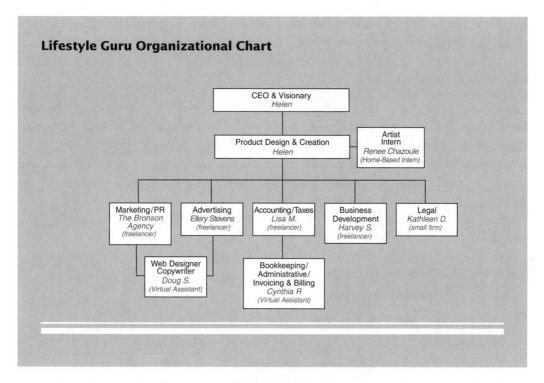

Lifestyle Guru Organizational Chart

Chapter 57. Planning to Outsource and Get More of a Life: Your Assignments for Days 14–16

The chart in the sidebar should be an example of how you can set up your business so that you are doing the important—and fun—work while the rest of the grunt work is being taken care of by competent professionals.

I want you to get there as well. Here's how:

Day 14: Create your own organizational chart. Right now your name will be in nearly every box, but begin thinking about what you want to do and what you can get rid of. Choose jobs you can outsource now and jobs you would like to outsource in the future. That will be your goal.

Days 15–16: Create a checklist for every job you want to outsource. The checklist should be detailed, but not overly fancy. Don't waste your time making it look like a manual—just get it down on paper. Your checklist should go over the exact tasks you want the new person to do.

You should write down: (1) Each job you want them to do, (2) Specific step-by-step instructions on how you want the job completed, (3) Anything you need to do to help them get up to speed, and (4) A timeframe for getting it done. Keep in mind you will not be able to forecast the amount of time for some skilled jobs, like web design and writing a press release, so negotiate a fee for the whole project and let the freelancer worry about how many hours it takes.

For example, let's say you are hiring a bookkeeper. The checklist might look like this:

Jobs for the New Bookkeeper:
Send out July invoices to retainer clients.

1. **Pull up the folder labeled "Client List" on the computer desktop.**
   When you open the file, you will see an alphabetized contact list in a spreadsheet. Every client's name and information are listed there. You will notice that the retainer clients are listed at the top of the page and are in red print. This first batch of invoices will go only to this group of clients. Next to each client name is a number, a dollar amount per hour, and a month. This is the number of hours we worked for them, the amount per hour we are billing, and the month we are billing.

2. **On the same desktop, there is a folder labeled "Invoice Templates."**
   In this folder is a copy of the invoice we use for our clients. You will see that we use the same invoice for every client and simply change the information (name, amount of the invoice, and date). Fill in these blanks using the information from the spreadsheet.

3. **After you've completed filling in the invoice, please double check the figures and print it.**
   Do the rest the same way. When you are finished with all of them (there will be ten in total for the month of July), please send them by messenger to my office for review.

4. **This job has usually taken me 2½ hours or so, but I understand this will take you a little more time until you get up to speed.**
   If this job is taking more than 3 hours, give me a ring at (212) 555-1212 and we can talk through some of the details. I would like to have the invoices in my office by the end of the day.

You get the idea. The checklist will be your guide and will help you get your new virtual employee up to speed. Just think, the more time they spend doing this stuff, the more time you get to live your life!

The Wrap Up: Days 1–16

WRAP-UP

VO Search #1...

Day 1: (Chapter 10) Be clear that you have a Home Office From Hell and are ready to change your business. Take the quiz and find out who you are—either a Lifestyle Guru or a Growth Maven.

Day 2: (Chapter 45) Look through the Yellow Pages, do an online search, scan the classified real estate sections of your local newspapers, and scroll through the listings on Craigslist.

Day 3: (Chapter 45) Once you've completed your search and narrowed your list of executive suites in your preferred locations, start calling them to find out what virtual office space packages they offer and ask about prices.

Day 4: (Chapter 45) Narrow your list to no more than your five top choices and make an appointment to tour each location.

Day 5: (Chapter 45) You should be able to visit all five locations in one day.

Day 6: (Chapter 45) Sign the agreement and pay any up-front fees (security deposit, etc.).

Day 7: Start using your new VO!

Or VO Search #2

Day 2: (Chapter 45) You can go to GetAVirtualOffice.com.

Days 3–7: (Chapter 45) You're done! This method buys you five extra days to make more money, develop something new for your business, get to the beach, or just kick back with a glass of wine and enjoy a little extra free time.

Day 8: (Chapter 53) Make a general, sketchy list of which time-sucking jobs you want to delegate, and how many hours you currently devote to these chores.

Day 9: (Chapter 56) Find yourself a good virtual staffing agency on the Internet.

Day 10: (Chapter 56) Contact the virtual staffing agency and discuss your specific needs and goals.

Day 11: (Chapter 56) Finalize paperwork with the agency. Phone your new VA and say, "Hi."

Day 12: (Chapter 56) Create a list of time-sucking jobs you will give to your VA with specific instructions, and your time expectations for each task. Send it to your new VA and follow up with a phone call. Set up a work schedule with your new VA.

WRAP-UP

Day 13: (Chapter 56) Get on to more important revenue-generating work.

Day 14: (Chapter 57) Create your own organizational chart.

Days 15–16: (Chapter 57) Create a checklist for each of the jobs you want to outsource.

Part 5

Calling All Lifestyle Gurus And Growth Mavens!

It's Time to Become a Nexpert!

"I like thinking big. If you're going to be thinking anything, you might as well think big."

–Donald Trump

Chapter 58: It's Time to Start Thinking Big...

Are you still with me? Great. Now comes the fun part.

The next two sections, "How to Become a Nexpert 101" and the more advanced section aptly named "How to Become a Nexpert 102," will help you use your successes from the last couple of weeks as a platform to become a recognized authority in your field.

I know. I know. You already know your job better than anyone else, right? Well, it's not enough to be an authority—you must be recognized as one.

In 101, you'll do three things: (1) Write a 500-word article and get it published in a trade journal or local newspaper, (2) Prepare a talk and set up two speaking engagements in your community, and (3) Create a Tips Booklet as a handout for your business.

In 102, you'll go even further. You will: (1) Create your own press release and set up two interviews with the press and (2) Create a tele-seminar. These accomplishments will get you *visible! Sayonara* Home Office From Hell!

You can't build the business of your dreams and remain the best-kept secret in your industry.

We're gonna change that...today!

Chapter 59. What the Hell Is a Nexpert?

Okay, I made this one up.

I made up the name but the concept is a sturdy and trusted one in the marketing arena.

A *Nexpert* is my terminology for a *niche expert*. A Nexpert is a person and/or business that focuses on a very narrow and specific customer base, and develops products, services, and marketing that are laser targeted directly to that customer base. An example is an accountant who specializes in working with homebased businesses, a PR consultant who works primarily with fashion industry clients, or a lawyer who primarily handles sexual harassment complaints in the garment district.

These people have a leg up on their competitors (who are simply accountants, PR consultants, and lawyers) because they are not generalists. They stand out because they have a narrowly defined specialty. They are experts in their field.

If you were having a dispute with a tenant and needed a lawyer, would you want any old lawyer or would you want a lawyer who specialized in landlord/tenant law? Of course, you want the expert because then you would be sure that they were up on the important case law that could help you win.

This is why becoming a Nexpert is crucial for your business. It will help you get noticed above the din. And whether you are a Lifestyle Guru or a Growth Maven, you want your business to be heard—loud and clear—in the marketplace.

Chapter 60. Why Nexpertizing Your Business Will Make All the Difference

Here's what you can do for your business as a Nexpert:

- Your specialization will help you stand out from the competition. It defines what you are and—by extension—what they are not.
- Customers will know something about you just because of how you define yourself, and they will have an easier time remembering you down the road.
- You will know exactly who your customers are, and can devise a marketing and advertising strategy to speak directly to them. Your plan can include promotions and ads customized for their eyes and ears.
- The narrower your niche, the easier it will be for potential clients to find you. ("Landscape Designer specializing in playgrounds, ball fields, and parks" is better than "Landscape Designer specializing in public outdoor spaces," which is still better than "Landscape Designer.")
- Advertising gets easier when you have a niche because you can target where your customers go online, or what they see or read. You can be right where they are.
- You can tailor your website to attract them because you will have an intimate understanding of what your customers want and what works for them.
- You will know what challenges your customers face, and your business can focus on devising products and services that will help them resolve those challenges.

■ This is a great chance for you to network your way into this community of customers, and be an active participant in their conferences, trade shows, and seminars.

Chapter 61. How to Become a Recognized Nexpert

I have an old friend named Harriet Delong who had a successful small business as a management coach. She has a Master's degree in Psychology, and counseled and cajoled CEOs and other executives at corporate-sponsored workshops and retreats. I worked with her at a retreat once and thought her techniques were brilliant, original, and effective. The companies that hired her loved her work, and the executives walked away feeling like they had gotten something valuable out of the experience.

But after 15 years of working with corporations, Harriet was tapped out and needed a change. She always dreamed that her business would move away from the corporate world and toward working with couples who needed help to strengthen their relationships, but unfortunately her business never really moved in that direction.

The final straw came at a corporate retreat she was working when two executives who were in a relationship took Harriet aside and asked her to help them with a work/love problem.

She continued working with them after the workshop and not only helped them with their issues, but she felt more fulfilled and happier than she ever did before. She realized again that working with couples was her passion.

I asked Harriet how she made the leap from executives to couples, and this is what she told me.

"Up until that time, when people asked me what I did or I had to describe my business, I would tell them that I worked with corporations and executives. That's what it said on my website and all my informational materials, so that is exactly the kind of work I got. I wasn't getting couples because I was running around telling people I worked with corporations," she explained.

"So, one day, I started saying, 'I host weekend retreats and workshops for married couples working through problems and hoping to get their relationships back on track.' I just kept saying it to anyone who asked, and three weeks later I had several full workshops planned and my website had been changed. It was as simple as telling people exactly what I wanted to do, as if I already did it."

That is the lesson here. The first step to becoming a Nexpert is *not* to read more books, sign up for classes, or decide that sometime next year—after you've gained more experience—you'll become one.

The time to start is today! All you have to do is start positioning yourself as one.

Chapter 62. Becoming a Nexpert: Your Assignments for Days 17–18

Day 17: Answer this question: What does your business do?

Make it short, sweet, and specific. Think as narrowly as possible—who are my customers, and what do I help them accomplish? Think about the people you want to serve, the business you want to have.

Fill in the blank: "My business helps…"

_____

_____

_____

Day 18: When people ask you about your business, tell them what you've written above and repeat it until it feels natural. Say it and repeat it until you finally accept that you are, in fact, a Nexpert!

Congratulations! You're officially a Nexpert.

Nexpert Story: Jimmy Alvarez

Jimmy Alvarez had a special gift. He had been an executive chef in several prominent San Antonio restaurants, but food wasn't his passion—saving restaurants from failure was.

"The failure rates of new restaurants are huge; well over 50 percent go under in the first year," he said. "I wanted to get out of the kitchen and give new restaurants a fighting chance."

Jimmy had seen firsthand how a few restaurants succeed and others fail. He had pulled several from the brink himself.

"It wasn't just about the food. It was about the behind-the-scenes stuff: how the menu was put together, how and from where the food was purchased, pricing, how the front-of-house staff interacted with customers, how the executive chef worked his kitchen. The factors were endless and so many businesses were clueless," he told me.

"They thought they could just open the doors and patrons would flood in."

Jimmy set up a very specific business niche. His business helped new, stagnating, and failing restaurants get on the path to success and profitability.

"Once I figured out who I wanted to help, I figured out a way to find them and talk to them."

He spoke at food industry events and gave out Tips Booklets at food industry conventions. He gave small, free, all-day workshops to fledgling restaurants in San Antonio, and targeted older restaurants that he felt could build on their longevity to create stronger businesses.

"I knew the more stable restaurants that wanted to modernize or increase performance and visibility could afford my fees. The businesses that were already hemorrhaging money could pay on a sliding scale with a bonus when and if performance improved. People are happy to pay if it is working," he told me.

"I also built in a maintenance program so restaurants could contact me for a small fee if they just wanted to check in about a problem that could be smoothed out with a little guidance, such as a staffing issue."

Jimmy's payment flexibility was proof that he understood the needs of new restaurants to keep costs down. His constant visibility at events made him a

continued

Nexpert Story: Jimmy Alvarez

trusted consultant. He was even dubbed "The Restaurant Whisperer" by a local journalist, and the title stuck.

"I became something of a food journalist, too—writing columns for industry magazines and the occasional article for the hometown newspaper. I also kept a daily blog that offered tips and hints. This underscored that I was an expert in saving restaurants, and the free tips were like giving someone a sample of my food—they could figure out immediately whether I would be able to help them or not."

Jimmy's success is a great example of how successful niche businesses work:

- *Have a very narrowly defined group of customers*
- *Know their needs*
- *Provide solutions for them*
- *Stay active and visible in their world (this is positioning)*

Chapter 63. Yikes! Am I Really Qualified to Be a Nexpert?

It's a little scary being a Nexpert, isn't it?

I remember when my first daughter was born and they told Barbara and me we could bring her home.

The first thing I thought was: "Are you crazy! You shouldn't let us take this kid home. We have no idea what we're doing! What the hell are they thinking giving us a helpless newborn?"

You may not feel like the consummate expert, but if you wear the hat—I promise, just as in parenting—you will rise to the occasion and fill those big shoes.

And really, you already know a lot about your business, don't you?

You know so much that when you were sitting in that ridiculous cubicle and listening to your hot-headed boss drone on endlessly in the umpteenth meeting of the day, you knew you had the determination and skills to do it better. And that's why you are here on your own.

So believe in yourself. Know that you don't have to know everything—nobody does. You just have to know more than your potential clients!

You are a Nexpert! Don't let anyone tell you differently.

Chapter 64. Let Me Say It Again

This is the plan that will help you become a Nexpert:

1. Have a very narrowly defined group of customers.
2. Know their needs.
3. Provide solutions for them.
4. Stay active and visible in their world (this is positioning).

Chapter 65. What Makes You the Nexpert, Jeff?

Great question! And here's the honest answer:

I'm a Nexpert because I positioned myself as one.

I'm a Nexpert because I took a chance and wrote this book. I didn't know everything before I started writing it—twice I completely changed the outline. But I became an even more knowledgeable and skilled Nexpert because of what I learned while I was writing.

I'm a Nexpert because I wrote a year's worth of columns for Inc.com, as well as articles for various newspapers and magazines around the country. However, before going to Inc.com, I'd never written a column, so I learned how to do it while doing it.

I became known as a Nexpert before I even realized I was one.

I'm a Nexpert because I get out there and speak to people and listen to the problems of homebased entrepreneurs. Then I create products and services that address those problems.

I'm a Nexpert because I have 34+ years of commercial real estate and small business experience. I feel I can take all the great stuff I've learned and use it to build my business and help other entrepreneurs build theirs.

I have a foundation of knowledge and experience—as you do in your field—and I did two things, both of which you can easily do.

1. I decided to position myself as a Nexpert, and I never second-guessed whether I deserved that title or not.
2. I did that by putting my knowledge and experience out there in interviews, speeches, columns, articles, and now a book. I became a recognized authority.

So here's the kicker: You can do it too.
And I'm going to show you how.

Get Thee to the Web!

I really shouldn't have to tell this to any small business owner in the 21st century, but if you don't have a website, you need to get one ASAP.

Not having a website is a little like not having your own telephone number.

Can you imagine telling your most important client, "Sorry, I can't do this conference call with London now," because the neighbors are talking on the party line?

It is so last century.

People are checking you out and want to easily search for you online. If they can't find you without much effort, they will stumble on to someone else who makes it easy for them to say "Yes!" There is always someone out there who wants to steal your business. Don't make it so easy for him.

A website is your face in the cyber world, and people will search for you online before they hire you or buy your product. They will want to get to your site and check out what you have to say, whom you've worked with, and what you are all about. This is your calling card and it gives you exposure—not only to your small town or city, but to the whole world. You cannot be considered a legitimate contender if you don't even make the effort of having a very basic website. This is also a great first place to start positioning yourself as a Nexpert by posting your bio and experience, and listing current and past clients, success stories, case studies, testimonials, press releases, interviews, articles you have written, and frequently asked questions (FAQs).

Also, please do not use a Gmail, Yahoo, Hotmail, or an AOL e-mail account for business purposes. No one will be impressed with your I'mASeriousBusinessReally @hotmail.com e-mail address.

Even your dear old granny in the nursing home has her own MySpace page and blog...get thee to the web! This is a no-brainer.

Part  6

How to Become a Nexpert 101

"The way to get started is to quit talking and begin doing."

—*Walt Disney*

Write One 500-Word Article And Get It Published in A Trade Journal Or Your Local Newspaper

"Only those who risk going too far
can possibly find out how far they can go."

—*T. S. Eliot*

Chapter 66. Why Getting Articles Published in Magazines, Newspapers, and on the Internet Will Help Grow Your Business

It's pretty simple—Having your name in print immediately positions you as an expert.

When you sit down at the computer and read a column on how to improve your business, and the columnist has written something that really hits home, you think, "Wow! What a great idea. I think I'm going to try that with my business."

And when you try that new thing and it really works, you can't help but think, "This guy had some great advice. He really knows what he's talking about. I'm going to read him again."

And so you go back and read his next column and he becomes one of those experts you respect and rely on for advice. When his book comes out, you pick it up. For the holiday season, you send a few copies to your colleagues, thinking they might get a boost from his ideas, too.

This guy is an expert because he's positioned himself as an expert, not because he has some kind of superpower that allows him to predict business success or profitability. And having his name on a website or in print in a newspaper or trade journal is independent verification that he must know something or maybe even a lot.

And we accept him as an expert—even though he is not a guru on a mountain, but a regular guy who has been out there and learned a few things and is willing to share them with other people.

Why shouldn't that be you?

Didn't I just describe you?

Consider a regular person who has been out in the marketplace and in the real world, building businesses, having successes and failures, learning how to do everything—sometimes the easy way, sometimes the hard way—and has learned a few lessons along the way.

That's you, right?

Now if you just share that information with other people, you too will be an expert.

Words In Print = The Truth

What did you read today?

Did you ask yourself, "I wonder if this story is actually true?" Of course not.

You—just as I and everyone else—just assumed it was true, because it was written in print.

Words have power. Once words are published in a media outlet, they convey a sense of authority. People almost never stop to question the veracity of things they read. They believe instinctively, "If someone printed this, it must be true."

What you say in an article for the print media will give you authority just by doing it. It is that powerful. So use the medium wisely with truthfulness, transparency, and integrity. But use it. Talk to your customers, craft a message, and start your own trend.

Chapter 67. Entrepreneurs Tell How They Got the Most Exposure Out of a Single Article

See what awesome things can happen for your business when you put yourself out there!

Amy Steenlin, pastry chef, Long Island, New York: "I wrote a 1,500-word article on the history and evolution of the cream puff and put a few of my recipe variations in for kicks. The article was published in a small local Long Island magazine and was seen by the editor of a very respected national food and wine magazine while she was there on vacation. I've done several articles for them now, and I do some kitchen and recipe testing for them as well."

Liza McKilligan, life insurance salesperson, Wilton, New York: "I wrote an article about a woman in our town who was left struggling financially with three children after her husband's death. He didn't have life insurance or much savings and she was left in dire straights. The story was touching and underscored the reason people should plan ahead for an accident or death of a family member. The article was published in a local newspaper in the weekend section, and I received a rush of phone calls and e-mails from people looking for life insurance. That was great for my business, but more importantly the exposure from the article inspired several local businesses to chip in to help the family. That was the best!"

Jon Wright, landscape designer, Fort Worth, Texas: "I wrote an article on crabgrass—believe it or not—for a hometown magazine. It was a funny piece, about 950 words, and it gave tips on getting rid of this lawn nuisance. The article ran in the spring issue, and from that one article I got 346 hits on my site and six new clients."

Neil Sarcum, photographer, Shreveport, Louisiana: "I wrote a 900-word article about how to take a good picture of your kids. Sounds silly, but most people don't know how to take pictures of their wiggly, constantly moving kids. The article, published in my local newspaper, was a hit with editors. Now I pen an article every month or so about photography and some aspect of Shreveport culture and they publish my pictures as well. Recently, a book publisher called me and is interested in doing a book. That little article really started a whole new career for me."

Mary Sen, nurse, Rockport, Maine: "I wrote an article for a nursing magazine about how patients can minimize their susceptibility to disease when they stay in the hospital. I did the article because an old nursing instructor of mine asked for the favor, but it turned out to be great. The article was seen by a local news anchor and I was asked to be a consultant on some of their medical stories—making sure they asked the right questions, got the facts right, etc. Now they ask me to speak on camera about different health issues. The whole experience has been incredible!"

You may not end up on the evening news, but articles can help you and your business become more visible.

Chapter 68. I'd Like to be Published in *The Wall Street Journal*—I Think

Are you already having dreams of being published in *The New York Times?* Looking forward to seeing your byline in *The Financial Times?* This is a lofty and possibly attainable goal, and it is a great clip to have on your website or in your portfolio. But you have to ask yourself:

"Is this the best placement for attracting new customers and making more money?"

A friend of mine who works in PR told me about an advertising client she had who wanted to be on Page Six. Desperately. Even though she got him great press in *Ad Week* and other respected industry publications, he wouldn't be satisfied until he got into the gossip column. After untold hours, she finally got him a mention. He was totally ecstatic, but as my friend told me, "Yeah, he was finally satisfied, but that little mention did absolutely nothing to help his business. The kind of companies that hire him are not looking for their ad agencies on Page Six."

It might be a sexy publication and great for your ego, but it's probably not the best placement for your business.

National papers may get you some attention, but if you are trying to create a niche in your town or city, you need to go where your customers are and that may or may not be a big publication.

Think about it. If you sell tractors and seed to farmers in Antelope, South Dakota (population 867), you need to be seen where the farmers will see you. That probably isn't in *The Wall Street Journal,* but it might be in the local newspapers, *The Farmers Almanac,* the weekly newsletter from the local supply store, and popular farm trade journals and Internet sites.

The point is that knowing your customer base is essential to your success as a Nexpert. You must also know where your customers are—what they read, what they watch, what they listen to—and tailor your strategy to speak directly to them.

Chapter 69. Who Is My Audience?

The first step to making sure your article writing—and any other marketing that you do—gets you the most benefit is to decide who your customers are. You must know who your audience is before you can write anything. So, let's figure that out now.

Remember, you are going for a small and specific group of people such as home-based businesses that need accounting and bookkeeping services, or independent retail stores looking for inexpensive, yet effective online marketing tools.

Define your customer base as specifically as possible. (Remember the Nexpert Story about Jimmy Alvarez, "The Restaurant Whisperer"?)

My customer base is...

_____

_____

_____

Chapter 70. Where Can I Reach My Audience?

So now that you know whom you are trying to reach, let's brainstorm some ideas about how to actually reach them.

What Internet sites are they going to (and where do you go)? Are there forums and blogs where people are talking about your area of business? The Internet is a great place to break into writing articles and columns because websites are always looking for fresh content.

What are the important trade journals in your business? Think about where your customers are going for information. Be there.

Don't be afraid to think small. Sometimes even a small chamber of commerce newsletter or a church bulletin—although not very sexy—can really pull in new clients and get the word out about your business.

Think about your local papers. Even having a piece in a small community newspaper will help you get noticed because people generally flip through these papers at breakfast and will notice someone from nearby or a name they recognize. If your clients are there, you should be there, too.

Now, make a list of specific publications you would like to target. This is your wish list of publications that would be a great venue for your first article.

1. _____

2. _____

3. _____

4. _____

5. _____

6. _____

7. _____

8. _____

Rearrange them so that your first choice is at number 1 and your last at number 8. After you write your article, you will contact each of these publications and pitch your article.

I'll show you how, but first, let's write the article!

Chapter 71. Know the Pubs Inside and Out

Okay, so you know your audience and where to reach them. Great!

But before you do anything else, get copies of the latest issues of these pubs and read them. Yes, you should know them inside and out.

You want to see what kinds of stories they publish and their writing style. Are the articles short and humorous? More just-the-facts-ma'am and informational? Are the editors looking for in-depth pieces or are they looking for short pieces with tips, hints, and how-tos?

Most magazine websites contain information about what kind of submissions are acceptable and even give you detailed information about how to contact editors. If it says, "No mail submissions," or "No stories about lost puppies," don't even think about it. It will be rejected on sight.

Most editors say the biggest reason for a rejection is that the writer didn't read the publication and didn't send something that was in line with their message and style. So read and get a sense of what they want before you hit the send button.

Chapter 72. Read about Writing

Everybody thinks they can write, but most people need help.

Make a small investment in yourself and get some good books on writing articles and columns for your business. I used a couple to get me started that I found very useful. I'll list them here to get you started. (No, I didn't write these books, the authors are not my friends, and I won't get any cash for recommending them. I just think these are worth the retail price.)

Cruise Amazon.com, BarnesAndNoble.com, or the bookshelves to find a couple that speak to you. Here are my top two picks:

1. *You Can Write a Column,* by Monica McCabe Cardoza
2. *Writer's Digest Handbook of Magazine Article Writing,* edited by Michelle Ruberg

Both of these books are published by *Writer's Digest.* Go to WritersDigest.com. They have a great assortment of books on writing, a free newsletter, lots of tips and articles on writing, a terrific magazine, and many other useful resources.

Chapter 73. Okay, Now I Have to Write Something—But What?

You know what your audience wants to read because you know them (you might even be one of them!), you know the places they go to for information, and you have researched what those articles and pubs look like.

Now, you must tackle the blank page.

Staring at an empty page sucks. There's no other way to say it. My advice is to try to avoid it whenever possible.

I do this by keeping a story file. Anytime an issue arises that makes me angry or makes a great point or is simply of interest to me and/or my clients, I clip it and put it in my file. (I do the same thing online by creating a bunch of files—one for each topic). That means when I sit down to write, I never have to ask what I should write about while I stare blankly at the screen.

There are always issues that pop up in your day-to-day work, or you suddenly find you have a creative answer to a problem that no one ever talks about. Whenever you find yourself thinking, "This is so simple—why doesn't anyone else do this?" run immediately to your story file and write it down.

Remember the last time you and your colleague got into a heated discussion over a beer after hours? Fodder for an article. Did you read that columnist who said something flat-out wrong and you want to set people straight? Fodder for an article. What about that new product that is selling like hotcakes but there are rumors of faulty construction?

This is where you should begin.

Write down one or two sentences that might make a great topic for an article. You might start and then find you've plotted out ideas for several articles. No worries—pick one and throw the extras in the story file for later.

Think about what your customers will want to read or find helpful and interesting, not what makes you look good or what you like. Remember that everything you write down can be erased, so don't worry about getting it perfect. Just get your ideas on paper.

Great Idea #1

_____

_____

_____

Great Idea #2

_____

_____

_____

Great Idea #3

_____

_____

_____

Great Idea #4

_____

_____

_____

Chapter 74. How to Pitch

Know the publication. Do your research.
This one is so big I devoted all of Chapter 71 to this subject. It will make or break you.

Take a look at editorial calendars on the pub's website.
These calendars give readers a heads up as to what issues are coming down the pike. Keep these upcoming topics in mind when you're pitching, and be sure to mention

that you have a great story about how to properly clean a gas grill for their upcoming summer issue.

Think ahead!

Don't pitch a Christmas story in November. Think at least three months ahead, because editors are thinking three months ahead.

Avoid looking like a novice, even if you are one!

Don't send unfinished articles or teasers. Get a copy of their guidelines on the web and follow them.

Find the right editor.

If you want to write a story about politics, don't waste time making your pitch to the crafts editor. Find the right editor and call the magazine to make sure the name listed on the website is still current. Also find out their exact name with the correct spelling. Don't address it to "Dear Sir/Madam" or "Dear Business Editor."

Pick up the phone.

Take your article idea right to the decision-maker. Look up the editor online and call. Many editors like to get a sense of the writer and the idea so they can ask questions and get clarification. Make sure you come to the pitch with a fully formed, thought-out, well-researched idea for the article. Editors are not going to work with you if they hear, "well…um…it's something along the lines of…maybe…how washing machines have revolutionized…you know…the lives of…um…people…kinda."

Submit a pitch for your article.

Make sure you tell the editor who your audience is, your experience, and any research that supports your pitch. The preliminary phone call should help both writer and editor steer the article toward a place where it will work best for the publication. If the editor wants a proposal, write a one-page (only one-page) proposal. If it takes you three pages, you will look like a novice. When you submit the pitch, editors can tell you what they would like to see from you, and you can construct the proposal based on that conversation. Unsolicited articles almost never get in.

Work with the editor.

Editors are there to help you. This is their job and most know how to do it well. Listen to them and trust their judgment. Also expect them to make changes to your piece.

It will happen, so make peace with it. You are not F. Scott Fitzgerald. You are look-ing to grow your business. As long as they are not changing the meaning or intent of your piece, it should be fine. If you cannot make a deadline and need more time (try to avoid this if humanly possible), pick up the phone and call. Most likely, all will be fine.

Face it; you will get rejected.

You will get rejections—so did Hemingway, Poe, J.K. Rowling (author of the *Harry Potter* series), and Mark Victor Hansen and Jack Canfield (who wrote the *Chicken Soup* series). So what? Don't get mad and wonder why *Tractor Pull Monthly* didn't get your unique brand of genius. Move on to the next pub on the list. If you aren't being rejected, you aren't in the game!

Nexpert Story: Jane Schwartz

 Jane Schwartz is a maternity clothing designer. Her boutiques are well known and popular in Minneapolis, her hometown, but Jane wanted to sell her clothes in New York, Chicago, and Miami. She is a Growth Maven if I ever saw one.

"Minneapolis was where I had always lived, so establishing myself there was easy. I knew everything I needed to know instinctively about the people there be-cause I am one of them," she said.

"I knew I was ready to take my clothes nationally, but I had no fan base out there. I wasn't even sure how to find them."

When we spoke, I suggested she think about starting a national dialogue in-stead of a local one. Jane was very active and visible in Minneapolis, but was virtu-ally unheard of outside the Midwest. We created a step-by-step plan for expanding her conversation with potential customers and buyers outside of Minneapolis.

First, we decided whom she wanted to target.

She decided to focus on upwardly mobile, educated, urban women between the ages of 25 and 40, who were either having or planning to have babies.

Then, we did some research. We found a list of publications these women

continued

Nexpert Story: Jane Schwartz

were reading, as well as blogs and websites. We narrowed that list down to eight media outlets we felt really personified the kind of customer who would appreciate Jane's hip urban designs and would be willing to pay the boutique prices.

Then Jane put together a column and pitched it to the editors.

"It took me two weekends to write," she said, "but most of the time was spent just trying to figure out one topic to write about. I wanted to say everything in one column."

She figured it out and found she loved writing. She put together two columns of about 750 words each. Then she called the editors on her list.

Two editors loved her writing but already had someone writing a column on a similar topic. Another felt that Jane's writing was too sophisticated for their readers. Another, a national maternity and parenting magazine, wasn't accepting columnists, but asked her to pitch them an article. (She did a month later and her article idea was accepted.)

Two editors never returned her calls. One loved her writing and asked her to complete a piece she was working on about looking stylish while pregnant and working; that article was published in their online magazine. The last editor—of a huge urban website for hipster moms—thought she was a perfect fit and asked her to write a blog for them.

"The column never panned out," Jane said, "but I'm writing a blog on this site that is seen every day by my core customers, thousands of them across the country. I'm answering their questions, talking to them, and selling my clothes. My online business is through the roof, and I'm opening small stores in two of my goal cities next year."

I'll say it again: publishing your ideas automatically positions you as a Nexpert. You can't be found if people don't know you are out there.

Chapter 75. Wait a Minute—I'm a Horrible Writer!

If you've tried writing and you hate it, don't have time for it, or aren't very good at it, then take my advice from the last section of this book and outsource it. Hire a competent ghostwriter.

There is no shame in hiring someone else to do it for you.

You know all those celebrity tomes out there? In many cases a ghostwriter wrote it. Ever wonder how someone who is nearly illiterate in a TV interview wrote that brilliant book? A ghostwriter wrote it. Ever wonder how those unbelievably busy CEOs made the time to jot off their memoirs? Ghostwriters wrote them.

Ghostwriters are used all the time, and they can be helpful in a myriad of ways—from helping you get your thoughts together, editing your finished work, going over your writing style, or writing the whole thing from cover to cover.

Just make sure you have a competent attorney—preferably one who specializes in literary works and copyright issues—put together a contract that spells out all the details. You should clearly state that your arrangement is on a work-for-hire basis, that you own all copyrights on any material that the writer writes for you, and that you may use that material in any manner that you choose. You should also spell out whether you want to keep your ghostwriting arrangement a secret or not.

Most ghostwriters will charge you less if you allow them to be acknowledged as a co-author, because those additional credentials will help them get more jobs. If you want them to keep your secret, you'll pay more. But that might be better for your business if you don't have to share the limelight with someone else.

After all, you want to establish yourself as the Nexpert, not your ghostwriter!

Just Get Published—The Money Will Come Later

Don't expect to make money for your articles. You won't get paid much or at all, but that isn't the point. Your published articles get you and your business out in front of your audience and give you credibility as an expert; it's not about getting an extra buck or two in your pocket.

When editors tell you there is no pay, just say, "No problem!"

Then, get excited when you see your byline because you will officially be a Nexpert!

Chapter 76. Why No Good Writing Goes to Waste

If you write 12 columns for a trade magazine next year, you won't simply have 12 pieces of writing. You may have the beginning chapters of a book.

Add to that the blog you've been writing, plus your other articles, and all of a sudden you have assembled a lot of information.

People say that once you get something published, it lasts until the paper is thrown out the next day, but that cliché was born before the Internet and before the search engines started collecting, categorizing, and storing everything forever.

Articles can be republished in different publications; columns and blog entries can be assembled into a book; old published articles can be archived on your website. Nothing you write goes to waste. It all can morph into something new!

The writing process is time-consuming and difficult, but you will reap so much from it.

Keep writing!

Chapter 77. Getting Published and Becoming a Nexpert Author: Your Assignments for Days 17–41

Day 17: Answer the question, "What does your business do?" in Chapter 62.

Day 18: Start talking like a Nexpert. When people ask you about your business, tell them what you've written (above) and repeat it until it feels natural.

Day 19: Decide who is your niche audience. Complete the worksheet in Chapter 69. Buy some books about writing articles for magazines and newspapers.

Day 20: Research where these customers are getting their information from and complete the worksheet in Chapter 70.

Day 21: Research these publications. Find out what kind of stories are being written and are of interest to your audience.

Day 22: Read about writing.

Day 23: Brainstorm ideas for stories, start an idea file, and continue adding ideas as you go along.

Days 24–26: Create a pitch for the article and begin to call editors.

Day 27: Call more editors and refine the pitch.

Day 28: Keep calling until someone likes your idea and wants to work with you.

Days 29–30: Create a one-page proposal of your article based on your conversation with the editor.

Day 31: Refine your proposal and send it to the editor.

Days 32–38: Begin writing (or start looking for a ghostwriter). Call back editor(s).

Days 39–40: Ask for feedback. Take criticism. Make edits.

Day 41: Submit to editor.

Retain Your Rights!

Before you can republish or reuse any of your articles that have been published by someone else, you need to make sure that you have retained all your copyrights and did not give them away to the publisher. Once again, this is where having a good attorney comes in handy. Retention of these rights needs to be negotiated upfront with the publications. In some cases they will agree to let you retain your rights; in other cases they will want all or most of those rights. You will need to weigh the pros and cons of getting your article/column published vs. keeping your rights so that you can use those articles again. If you plan to write a book and those articles will be an integral part of that book, you will want to keep those rights. If getting published in The New York Times or Fortune Magazine might propel your business to new heights, then it may very well be worth giving up your rights in that case. You need to make these decisions on a case-by-case basis.

Set Up Two Speaking Engagements

*"According to most studies, people's number one fear is public speaking.
Number two is death. Death is number two. Does that sound right?
This means to the average person, if you go to a funeral,
you're better off in the casket than doing the eulogy."*

—*Jerry Seinfeld*

Chapter 78. Why Speaking Is Almost Always Worth the Effort

Do your palms start to sweat when you think of yourself at the podium? Do you have to do that thing where you think of everyone in their underwear before you do a presentation?

Speaking can make anyone turn clammy, but here is why speaking is worth conquering your fears: As soon as you stand in front of that audience and open your mouth, you are considered a Nexpert.

It makes you credible. Think about it. You might be the guy in the audience who knows more than anyone else, but unless you are standing in front of people showing them that you are the guy who knows more than anyone else, they won't know it and you won't get credit or respect for it.

Speaking also allows you to come out of your office cave and meet people face-to-face. When audience members listen to your talk and hear you come up with answers to their questions, they are getting to know you in a personal way. They are seeing you in action. They are seeing what your company can do for them.

When they hear you make a joke, entertain them, keep them intrigued, regale them with relevant stories, or make a point that turns on the light bulb in their heads, it tells them something about who you are and what your business is all about.

Face it—people do business with people they trust, and there is no better way to gain people's trust than by showing them who you are, up close and personal.

Chapter 79. I'm Afraid to Speak in Public. Can I Really Do This?

Okay, it's terrifying.

I won't argue with you about that. I have my own set of demons that rear their ugly heads every time I step in front of an audience. If you put me on *Good Morning America* and I knew that 3 billion people had just tuned in, I wouldn't even give it a second thought. But stick me at a podium in front of 15 people, and my palms start to sweat profusely and I can barely remember my own name.

Turns out I'm great in interviews and any kind of Q&A where I'm just answering questions, telling stories, and yammering on about business. But the formal stuff—the 20-minute prepared speech—is a grueling, stammering exercise for both the audience and me.

So I've learned to do what I'm good at. I've learned to stick to my strength, which is that freewheeling, chatty type of talk. I have thrown away my prepared speeches and I now pepper my talks with lots of Q&As. I try to encourage a lot of audience participation because I know that's when I'm hot, and I can really help people and show my businesses in a good light. I will never go back to the prepared speech because there really isn't enough alcohol in the world to make that ever happen again!

I know all this because I just went out there and did it. I took my speech and bombed more than a few times. I stood there facing those blank, bored, unimpressed faces and decided to do it again.

I can't tell you how tough that is.

And then, I had a bunch of successes. I spent time figuring out what worked and what didn't. I tried it and kept trying. I didn't like the failures but I tried not to be afraid of them. I figured out what my strengths were and I started playing to them.

The times I bombed never had an impact on my business or the bottom line— these were merely opportunities to learn and get in touch with my humility!

The point is that what can be gained is so much bigger than what you can lose. Stretch yourself. Go for it!

Chapter 80. How to Create the Best Speaking Opportunities for Your Business

We all have those potential clients we know we could bag—if we could just get in front of them.

Well, imagine you now have your chance.

Imagine being in a room full of people in your niche and having their undivided attention. Imagine being able to talk about your business and give them a little taste of what makes you so great. Imagine them understanding exactly how you could help their business, and then doing it!

That's what can happen when you are a speaker. You need to find the opportunities that will get these results. You can't just speak anywhere. And not every opportunity is a good opportunity.

Here are some things to think about when you are deciding where you should be demonstrating your Nexpertise!

Your audience should be fish in a bowl.

Remember you are a Nexpert—so think small. Think about your niche. The best speaking engagements are the ones that get you right in front of your niche audience.

Want to get in front of carpenters in your city? Speak at the Carpenters Union. Want to speak to small business owners in your county? Contact the Chamber of Commerce, the Masons, the Small Business Association of your town. Want to find vacuum cleaner salespeople? Try the Vacuum Cleaning Conference at the local Holiday Inn.

Don't worry about speaking at that huge national conference where you might have an audience of 500 but only a handful are in your niche. You'll get more bang for the buck if you go to the small place where the audience holds exactly the people you want to reach.

Know how many people are going to be there.

So, you know who is going to be there, but you have to decide how many potential clients you can get from the time and energy you put into crafting a presentation and giving it.

Is it worth your time to speak to less than 30 people? Maybe it would be very beneficial to speak in front of ten people if they are the right ten people. Think about your target audience and make sure those people are in the room. If they are the right people, even a handful of them might make for a great opportunity.

Get some feedback about the venue.

Who else has spoken at this meeting and what was their experience like? Does the organization give speakers adequate support and facilities? Will they allow you to make decisions about how long the talk will be or whether there'll be a Q&A session? Will there be an open bar and will the audience be a bit inebriated? Will yours be the last speech after a long day of seminars? This information is important and will help you tailor a talk that will work well for the audience and for you.

Go on the hunt.

Look in advance through trade magazines and industry websites for upcoming meetings, conferences, expos, and conventions to see what events might be a great showcase for your business. Think about your favorite industry events—the ones you've always attended as a participant—and think about applying as a speaker. Most conference organizers can send you a package that will help you get all the materials together to apply or will provide the application on their site.

Also, keep any direct mail you get about conferences. There might be great opportunities for you to get yourself on a panel. A panel is a great way for you to be a Nexpert without having to actually go to the trouble of writing a speech. You just answer questions and give commentary—this is definitely my favorite!

Plan early.

It is good to get on the mailing lists of your favorite event organizers. That way you'll know what they are doing early on, and you can make decisions about what venues are best for your business. National events plan nearly a year in advance, regional events about half that, so think ahead. The earlier you put together a proposal, the better your chances of being accepted. It pays to be the early bird.

Recycle.

You can recycle your speeches if you have a real winner. Just remember to update them. Your speech may be great, but if you make a joke about Ronald Reagan's last trip to Russia, you may let the cat out of the bag! Stay current and keep adding fresh material to your old speeches.

You Are Not Selling. You Are Teaching.

Even though your end game is getting more clients, making more money, and improving your business, you can never make your talk about that.

Your role once you write that column or step up to the podium is that of a teacher. You are there to help people grow their businesses.

You are there for the audience.

If your speech is all about you or reads like one of those endless, sales-oriented marketing letters, people will stop listening and dismiss you as a fraud.

You can sell more vacuum cleaners by teaching people about dust than you can by telling them about your great machines.

Chapter 81. Cool Things You Can Get for Your Business Because You Are the Speaker

Being a speaker has its perks.

Decide what things are important to you and try to make them happen. At the end of the day, you are doing this to get new business. If the speaking engagement won't get you new business, don't do it. You have better things to do with your time. Move on to the next and better opportunity.

Remember that speaking and writing articles are marketing expenses. Some conferences may offer you a small honorarium, but this is not about making a piddling amount of money for your speech—this is about becoming a Nexpert and having a stronger business with new and better clients.

I suggest you tell the organizer you will forgo your fee in lieu of a perk or two. These perks could help grow your business and be far more valuable than a small check.

Here are a few ideas:

- See if the organization will give up a list of its members. That way you can send them e-mails and promotional materials that will promote your business.
- Create a free Tips Booklet, which you will learn about in Chapter 90, and ask people to provide their name and contact info (their business card).
- If you are speaking at a regional or national conference, the organizers will send out packages of promotional information about the event to everyone who is attending. Make sure you get your brochure in there. Also, if that package will have a newsletter or magazine, see if they will reprint an old article of yours. Tell them this will help members get a feel for your talk and they might just go for it.
- Organizers of smaller venues and associations like the personal touch, so ask for the e-mail addresses of the participants beforehand, and send them a worksheet or quiz you want them to fill out and send back to you before they come. This whets their appetite and spreads the word about you. It also helps you develop a more personal relationship with people before you even walk in the room. That will make you feel more at ease and the audience will feel like they got more out of it.
- See if you can talk someone into letting you get a few free ads in their conference newsletter or magazine. Tell them to forgo the charge for the ad and you will forgo the charge for the speech.
- Get lists of the organization's state, regional, or local chapters and the name and contact info for the meeting organizers. That way you can give the same talk to more people in the same industry.

Chapter 82. Who Is Your Audience? What Makes Them Tick?

I've asked you this question before in the article writing section, but I can't stress how important the answer is for everything you present to the world.

Want to buy your husband a gift that will make him ecstatic? You better know him inside and out. You better know what makes him tick. Want to prepare a presentation that makes a certain client sit up and notice you? You better know what makes her tick.

Want to make an audience roar with laughter and then come up to you after your speech and request more information about your company? You better know what makes them tick. Want an editor to see there is a book in your blog? You better know how the book business ticks.

You shouldn't ever put fingers to the keyboard without knowing who is going to read you or listen to you, because everything comes from knowing your audience.

What does your audience care about? Are they looking for cold, hard facts and figures they can jot down in their notebooks? Are they medical patients who are emotionally involved in what you will be saying? Do they need support as well as information?

Is the room filled with people who are already suspicious of you and need a little nurturing to bring them into the fold? Should your speech be designed to build trust and tear down barriers? Does the audience want inspiration or information?

Is your audience a group of people who might appreciate storytelling and the occasional joke? Or are they looking for no-nonsense answers to pressing questions? Will they be tense or enjoying a drink while they listen to you? Are they more likely to want to hear verbose, academic language or short, clear sentences? Would they have a better experience with a two-hour seminar or a 20-minute speech and a generous Q&A session?

These are just a few questions to start asking yourself. But know this; you cannot get your message across unless you know your audience. Try this:

Who is my audience?

_____

_____

_____

Now, think like your audience and ask yourself, "What would my audience like to see from me and my presentation?"

_____

_____

_____

Chapter 83. What Message Do You Want Them to Get?

If a member of the audience went out into the foyer directly after your talk and could be heard commenting on your talk, what would you want them to say about you and your message?

"I just heard Jim's talk in there and it was excellent! He told us…"

_____

_____

_____

"But it wasn't just what he said, it was how he told us, he…"

_____

_____

_____

Don't step up to the podium before you know the answer to these questions.

People know when it isn't clear what you want to say. They know when you are beating around the bush or your talk isn't cohesive.

They know when you don't know. So answer this:

"I want the audience to learn that…"

_____

_____

_____

This is the core of your talk. Everything you say and do is in service to this message.

Chapter 84. What Is Your Intention?

You know your audience and you know what you want to tell them. Now, I want you to find the best way to get that message across.

This is the tone and intention of the talk. There are several, and these are well documented in most speaking how-to books. You should know what your intention is for your talk.

Do you want to sell people a new blender? Get them up to speed on new blender technologies? Share and get some new ideas about how to solve old blender problems? Do you want to teach them how to repair an old blender? Do you want to inspire them to go back to blender school?

Each of these intentions is different from the others, and if I gave a talk about each of these blender topics, each one would sound completely different, even if we talked about the same thing. Why? Because your intention will dictate the tone of your speech.

You can choose to make a speech that has more than one intention; for instance, you can teach and inspire. The point is your intention will impact how you prepare your talk.

What Is Your Intention?

If your intention is to:	Your speech will:
Entertain & Get People Interested	Be funny, whimsical & loaded with stories
Teach & Inform	Give people concrete tools
Excite & Inspire	Motivate them & use strong inspirational phrases
Persuade & Sell	Send a strong message about the product
Get Feedback & Explore New Ideas	Open the floor to other people's ideas
Establish Credibility & Respect	Be authoritative, confident & knowledgeable

So what is your intention? Pick one of the above. Then, tailor your talk to match the tone.

My intention is to...

_____

_____

_____

Chapter 85. Get Their Attention—Repeat the Message

Speechwriting is so much about these two things: You can't get the audience's attention unless you have a great message, and you can't get them to hear your great message unless you get their attention.

How's that for the chicken and the egg?

Speechwriting sounds daunting, but like so many disciplines of writing, there is a formula for getting it done well. Your speech will always have three sections—the beginning, middle, and end. Here are the functions of each:

Start off hot.

The beginning of your speech has to grab the audience's attention. Don't start off with boring facts or an obscure chart. There are several ways to go here:

1. Grab them with a great joke that humorously (and tastefully) introduces the point of your talk. "A priest, a rabbi, and a carpenter are sitting at the bar..." (Only choose humor if you are sure you can tell a joke under pressure.)
2. Open with an engaging story that makes your point: "Let me begin my talk by telling you what I learned from staying at a monastery for two weeks."
3. Ask the audience a question: "How many of you out there hate your jobs?"
4. Begin with an exercise or quiz. "Before we start, I'm going to make you take a little test. Let's see how many of you are really living up to your potential."

5. Have the audience make the first move: "Let's see who's in our audience today. Stand up, tell us your name and a little bit about why you want to start a home-based business."

Then, after your engaging opening, you need to make your point. This is the core reason for the whole talk—the message you want to send them. Tell them straight out and make your introductory story, joke, or exercise support that message.

Pepper the middle with facts that support your point.

The middle is important but less important than the beginning and end. The middle is where you use facts and supporting evidence to back up your message.

If you are trying to make the point that moms can earn money for the family and still work from home in their own business, the middle section is where you supply the details. You can discuss how they can keep their startup costs low, how they should handle childcare, and what supplies and materials they will need.

All of these details are in service to the bigger message, which is to inspire and teach moms how to start their own homebased businesses! So make sure your tone is both inspirational and informational.

End with a bang and a call to action!

Think of your ending as a bookend. You should refer back to the first story or example in your introduction. "Remember we started today with the mom who had five kids and no income and she started her dog-grooming business in her garage? Well, now she has 23 dog-grooming supply stores in the Bay area and a million bucks in her bank account. And you can do it too!"

This makes the speech feel complete—we started with an idea and we finished with that same idea. You want your ending to be memorable and also to inspire people to act. There are no facts and figures here—just getting people out of their seats to do something. Maybe you want them to buy your product, or sign up on your direct mail list, or pick up your handout, or just think about changing their lives.

Whatever it is, the ending should get the audience to act on your words.

Start with a Trick

I have a friend named Janice Hames who used to teach a lunchtime business-writing workshop at the local bookstore. She wrote business-writing books and this was a great way for her to market herself to potential readers.

She chose bookstores in business districts because her target audience was people who wrote for business every day and struggled with it. People popped in during their lunch hour (or they might already be in the bookstore) and got a free and quick (20 minutes) lesson on some aspect of business writing and some freshly brewed coffee.

Janice always kept her latest book on the table in front of her, and the bookstore provided signage about her book, but she never once mentioned it or tried to sell any copies. Instead, she got people to buy her book by using a little trick. She claimed she could improve anyone's e-mail writing in just 20 minutes and she would provide proof.

This is brilliant, of course, because we all use e-mail every day, and we all secretly wish we could articulate ourselves better in e-mail, but taking a class is not a priority. This idea is also something that grabs the audience's attention and keeps them interested because they are only investing 20 minutes. They have nothing to lose. In fact, many people who attended her workshops were people who happened to be in the bookstore by coincidence and were intrigued by this idea.

Janice started by giving the audience a scenario—something like, "You drove to work this morning and it was pouring rain. You found that the new guy had parked in your spot for the third time and you had to walk seven blocks in the rain, you were late to the client meeting, and your boss chewed you out."

Then, she would say, "Assuming that e-mail is the most appropriate form of communication, write the new guy an e-mail."

She took no questions and asked people to just write for seven minutes. After they had finished, she gave them four simple rules they should think about when writing any kind of e-mail. Then, she had them rewrite the e-mail, keeping in mind the four rules they just learned.

continued

Without fail, every person, every time, saw that when they followed her tips, their second e-mails were immensely better. The whole lesson took less than a half hour and she proved she could change their writing in that amount of time.

She sold books at every session, and the lunchtime series helped her sell more spaces at her full-day workshops and pick up corporate clients.

The point is she had a trick, a gimmick—and not just any gimmick, but one that delivered results quickly and made a good impression. You don't have to beat people over the head to get them to buy your products, just show them how you can make their lives better and they'll bite every time.

Chapter 86. The Marvelous Q&A

The Q&A is, arguably, one of the most important parts of any talk. I almost never make up my mind about speakers until I see how they do in the Q&A.

Why?

Because the prepared talk is highly stylized and edited. It is designed to carry the message. It can be rehearsed and rehearsed until all the freshness is drained from it.

What I want to see is how the speaker can apply his concepts to my situation.

The Q&A lets you speak directly to your audience. It lets you tackle their questions and concerns and come off looking like a pro. It allows you to go off script and show how you handle what you know. It allows your personality to come through and gives people a chance to see who you really are. Warts and all, as they say.

And that isn't a bad thing. The warts are just fine.

Your potential audience doesn't want to hire a mannequin with a perfect presentation. They want someone trustworthy, dedicated to service, and talented. If they think you can help them or their business, they'll take you—warts and all.

Don't be afraid to show who you really are in the Q&A. Here are some tips:

- Be transparent when people ask the tough questions. They'll respect you for the truth.

- Plan ahead if you know tough questions are going to be coming at you. Preparation is your best defense.
- Answer questions directly and head-on. Nothing is more infuriating than asking a question and having the speaker deflect it or launch into some diatribe. Listen to your audience.
- Be animated. Come out from behind the podium. Take off your jacket and loosen your tie. Sit on the edge of the stage. Walk around the room. This is an opportunity to get personal with your audience.
- Don't belittle anyone or make people feel bad for asking a question (even if they are trying to heckle or stump you). Being respectful and patient (and showing grace) will win you points with the rest of the audience.
- Just in case people are shy about being the first to ask a question, come with a question for them to get the ball rolling: "Why don't we start with you telling me about some of the problems you're facing getting roller skates off the store shelves?"
- Invite the audience to come up and speak with you after the event if they have any personal questions you might be able to answer. If you demonstrate that you are accessible, it sends a message that you are accessible in your business.

Chapter 87. Speak Like a Pro

Here are some tips from the pros on how to wow 'em with your talk:

- **Prepare your talk.** Whether it's a formal speech and you've memorized every word for a conference room filled with 200 people, or an extemporaneous talk at the local chamber of commerce, be prepared. Know your audience. Know the message you want to send. Know the best way to get that message across. That will make you feel more confident.
- **Make sure you know the material backward and forward.** The speaker ahead of you might cover something in your talk and you may have to make last-minute adjustments. Audience questions also may interrupt the flow of your speech, so knowing the material well will keep you from freaking out when disturbances come up.

■ **Start with a winner.** The first few minutes of a speech are crucial, so begin with a winner. Start with a story that always gets a positive reaction or a joke you tell brilliantly and can use to settle the house and cut the tension. But use a time-tested beginning. If you tell a lame joke or tell a good joke badly and it flops in the first 30 seconds, it will take you until the middle of the speech to recover. Start with something surefire.

Put Down the Pointer and Step Away from the PowerPoint!

Ask any competent speech coach or speechwriter and she will tell you that PowerPoint is one of the worst things to happen to public speaking since stage fright.

Yes, hundreds of thousands of businesses use it. You've probably sat through your share of dry, bullet-pointed presentations that all look the same. So I ask you, why do that to someone else? Are you a sadist?

PowerPoint can turn a dynamic, energized presentation—one that shows off the individual skills and unique charisma of the speaker—into a tedious, mind numbing, slide show of mediocrity.

You can't be new, different, or memorable while you are chained to those cryptic one-liners and pie charts.

Your event organizer may ask you to supply one, but you should not be bullied.

In fact, graphics are not necessary. These might lend themselves beautifully to your area of expertise. If so, use them, but you are under no obligation to supply graphics unless graphics really drive home the point or jazz up the talk.

If you must use PowerPoint, try not to use the slides through your whole talk. Instead, use them as a kind of example: "This chart shows just what I'm talking about—puppy sales have increased steadily over the last year."

The point is: If you must use them, use them sparingly. There is nothing worse than watching someone blunder through 60 slides while you are fine-tuning your grocery list and texting your wife on your Blackberry under the table.

- **Don't do anything that will distract you before your speech.** Don't take that call from your craziest, most infuriating client minutes before you walk out on the stage, and don't even think about opening that bill from the vendor who always over-bills you. These little distractions can alter your mood and drag you down. You want your mind to be clear and focused on the task if you want the presentation to go well.

- **Take a few breaths.** Believe it or not, a few deep breaths and a quiet moment can really help you get your mind in the right place. The more relaxed you are, the more relaxed your talk will sound.

- **Practice.** Practice speaking in front of colleagues and friends, on video, in front of the mirror, with a speech coach, whatever—but practice. A run-through with a few thoughtful critics will help you get a handle on whether you are shuffling your feet, waving your arms nervously, saying "uh" in every sentence, or scratching your chin compulsively.

- **Your body language speaks.** People will instinctively look at your gestures to read if you can be trusted. Nervousness can often be perceived as dishonesty.

- **Oh, and whatever you do, don't read!**

- **Make eye contact.** There is nothing worse than a speaker who is looking at the floor or the back wall. This is an opportunity to *connect* with people, so connect! There is always some lovely person in the first few rows who is smiling approvingly or nodding affirmatively at all your brilliant points.

Make eye contact with that person a lot, then, make eye contact around the room and keep coming back to that smiling, nodding person. It will give you confidence and help you make a real connection with the audience.

- **Keep it simple.** A good speech can be understood by both CEOs and interns. Don't go for dense and jargon-infested techno-speak. It won't impress and it won't win people over to your side if you make them feel stupid.

- **How you look counts.** The audience will make a judgment about you based on how you look—before you even open your mouth. So think about how you dress and what image you want to project.

- **Be flexible and change it up!** Don't be afraid to adjust your presentation style to different audiences. When I was in college, I had a friend in the philosophy department. She was pretty bright and the faculty asked her to teach a class on Kant to incoming freshman. She knew they wouldn't buy her as an authority figure, so she wore jeans and sat cross-legged on the professor's desk. They loved it. She knew if she tried to come off like a professor, they would've eaten her alive. Her teaching style was geared to reach her audience. The point here is to adjust your style to get the best reaction from the audience.

- **Match your tone to the content of your talk.** If you are speaking about how to live a more energetic life, you better not speak with a monotone drone. If you are talking about dying at home, you better not be making corny jokes and trying to get a laugh.

- **Monitor speed.** Keep track of how fast or slowly you are speaking. Most people talk faster when they speak because they are nervous or trying to get through it. Speaking too slowly can be a real bore for the audience and speaking too quickly makes it hard to take in your message. You want to be somewhere in the middle.

- **Pause.** Most professional speeches have the word "pause" written into the speech, for example, after making a big point or making a joke. This forces you to take a breath and slow down even when you are rolling on your speech. Taking a pause gives you and the audience a moment to just sit with the information before moving onto the next thing. Write the word "pause" into the body of your speech as a reminder.

- **Keep it short.** Is there anything more nauseating than a speaker who drones on and on past his time limit? You're good, but no one wants to listen to you talk and talk and talk. Keep it concise. Review your points before you conclude. Move on to the Q&A. Mingle with the audience after the event and make yourself available to folks who want to speak with you personally.

Chapter 88. How to Use Handouts to Seal the Deal

Handouts are a great way to make a lasting impression. It is something concrete in hand that audience members can take home, mull over, and flip through on the plane home. The idea is not to give someone a brochure, which is about marketing *you*, but to give them something that offers them tips, ideas, or things to think about while it summarizes your talk.

Remember, the handout should help people learn about dust with the idea that when they do that, they'll want to buy your vacuum cleaner.

The handout can be a single page outlining the top ten reasons you should have a website for your business. It can sum up your talk or—even better—go into detail about one area of your talk. This shows you are the Nexpert and reminds people of the speech without going over every detail. You can also provide a resource guide: your favorite books, DVDs, and speakers. Give each favorite a little summation so readers know why you like it and how it can work for them.

Or you can create a Tips Booklet—which I've mentioned before and will have you create in the next section—that is a 2–10 page booklet that outlines your thinking about a topic, like "Twenty Days to Becoming a Healthier, Happier Person."

This is a great way to help sell your yoga mats, clothes, and DVDs along with your special line of Omega 3–filled organic food. (Notice you aren't selling the organic food. You are selling the better, healthier life in the hope that they will trust you, buy your organic food, and do yoga on your specially designed mats.)

A great handout has some of the following characteristics:

- **Your contact information listed visibly and clearly:** Include your full name, business name, address, phones, website, and e-mail address.
- **Lots of white space:** This means you should not have big blocks of text and many images all squished onto a page of paper. The eye takes in more information when there are some blank areas. This book is good example of white space. Use bullets and lists as a way to impart information.
- **Concise language:** You don't have the space to blab on about your theories and ideas and all the things you want to do. Sum up your talk. Drive home your main message, and follow up with your call to action.
- **Effective call to action:** This is your chance to make something happen. Get people to your website. Have them win a Tips Booklet or a free product sample if they register on your site. Give them a discount if they join your mailing list at the seminar or bring the handout to your store. Use this as an opportunity to inspire immediate action.
- **Print the handout on colored paper.** That makes it stand out from all the other papers in their briefcase.

Nexpert Story: Bea Richardson

"I gave the worst speech on the planet," Bea Richardson told me. She runs a small travel agency in Las Vegas specializing in arranging tour packages and sightseeing activities for groups of tourists. She works closely with hotels and wanted to be more visible with hotel management.

She took my advice and started applying to hotel industry events and conferences as a speaker. She was accepted to several and started writing her talk.

"I was pretty confident going in. I had done a lot of speaking to tourist organizations trying to drum up business, but this was a different industry. I thought I could just waltz in there with the same old information and everyone would lap it up."

Bea spent some time working on her talk, but not nearly enough. She, like many of us, was happy to just get in there and wing it.

"I'm pretty charismatic and I teach at the local college. In my business, I'm talking all the time. I couldn't imagine not being able to handle a speaking situation," she told me.

Five minutes into her talk, someone from the audience questioned the entire premise of her speech. It knocked her completely off and she couldn't recover for quite awhile.

"I wasn't expecting to be so blatantly challenged—and right in the middle of my speech—it flattened me. I must have turned as white as a sheet. I know my mouth was hanging open. I remember searching through my notes frantically, and time seemed to slow down. Everything was quiet and really uncomfortable," she confessed.

"It was possibly the most embarrassing moment of my life."

Bea eventually recovered somewhat (after a lot of hemming and hawing), but it was never the same. She couldn't get her confidence back and never really regained the audience's respect. She cut the Q&A short and hightailed it out of there.

Bea was devastated, of course. It isn't fun to fail, and it's even worse to fail in public. But she learned a valuable lesson—you have to know your audience before

continued

Nexpert Story: Bea Richardson

you speak or draft that talk. You have to know who they are and what they need.

You can't simply recycle talks. You will be outed, usually by some loud-mouthed buffoon in the second row.

The experience wasn't a complete loss for Bea. She learned from it, and like a real pro, went back to do it again. She has since spoken at many hotel conferences and events and has never made the same mistake again. In fact, she no longer has to apply because they ask her to speak.

Bea keeps a file of articles and notes about her tourists and what they like to do. She continually updates her talks so she is on the cutting edge of information about the business.

"It isn't enough to be a good speaker. You have to be on the forefront of information. You have to say something new that the audience can take and use. Do that and it will make you a Nexpert in their eyes."

The proof is in the pudding; Bea's business has grown substantially and so has her bank account.

"Being perceived as an authority in your field makes people want to work with you."

Chapter 89. Giving Your Nexpert Talk: Your Assignments for Days 42–61

Okay, now you're going to get your feet wet. I want you to set up two speaking engagements.

Don't think national conferences (which take time and advanced planning). Focus on setting up talks with two small organizations in your area. These organizations— the Italian-American Small Business Forum, the Chamber of Commerce, the Knights of Columbus, and the Women's Business Alliance—are small enough to welcome speakers with great content while requiring less formality.

Keep in mind that the audience should be a group of people in your niche area.

Day 42: Fill in the blanks in Chapters 82–84. Decide on who your audience is, what message you want to send, and what kind of speech you will prepare.

Days 43–44: Research the best speaking opportunities in your area. Look for organizations that are rich in your niche target audience and qualify as great speaking opportunities (use the criteria in Chapter 80). Start making contact and call the organizers.

Day 45: Start outlining your talk and create a short, one-page proposal outlining what you will speak about, how long the talk will be, and the format in which you will deliver the talk (workshop, seminar, formal speech, etc.)

Day 46: Get together the materials to send to the organizers. This will include a short bio for them to send to attendees, a picture, and any other material that you feel helps position you as a Nexpert.

Days 47–49: Send out the proposal and information about you and your business by e-mail. Follow up with organizers after they receive your information. Call new ones and send them proposals. Be persistent.

Days 50–56: Write and prepare your talk. Keep talking to new and existing organizers. Set dates for talks and firm up details.

Day 57: Practice the talk in front of a mirror or camera. Critique yourself. Then give it to a practice audience or friend. Get feedback. Practice and work out the kinks.

Days 58–60: Rewrite and hone the speech. Practice giving the speech again to work out any final kinks, and have your practice audience throw questions at you for the Q&A session. Finalize speaking dates and go over last-minute issues.

Day 61: Keep going over the speech every few days until you speak. When the time comes, enjoy that you finally got what you deserve—you are a Nexpert speaker!

Create One Tips Booklet

"Every artist was at first an amateur."

—*Ralph Waldo Emerson*

Chapter 90. What the Hell Is a Tips Booklet?

A Tips Booklet is, as you might expect, a little book that houses tips and ideas.

Not exactly rocket science and that is really the point. You can create a great little piece of Nexpert marketing for your business over the course of a weekend with very little sweat equity!

Tips Booklets can be self published on any good printer, printed at your local print shop, or uploaded to your website. People can access it on your website as a PDF, for example, and spare you printing costs and labor.

Some people sell their Tips Booklets, for anywhere from $5 to $15. Other people prefer to give them away as a way to attract customers to their other products and services.

The booklets are—no surprise—small, generally 4" x 9" because that makes it easy to throw one into a standard business envelope and mail it off to potentially interested parties. Anything bigger than that and you're schlepping off to the post office for more stamps and bigger packaging.

The booklet is designed to be simple—something with minimal graphic design, colors, and photos. It is supposed to be something you can complete over the course of a few days and do it on the cheap.

This is not a brochure or a book, and its preparation should not be labor intensive. We're talking somewhere between 10 and 25 tiny pages, and the writing is not dense narrative that takes forever to prepare. Instead, the booklets provide lively lists of tips, strategies, ideas, and techniques that your customers can use to improve their life or their business. They are designed to be scanned, not read cover to cover.

Tips Booklets are for teaching and helping. This is not the place to hawk your wares or engage in some marketing rhetoric about how great your company is—Who wants to pay for that? This is your chance to give them "50 Ways to Organize Your Kid's Room and Keep it That Way" in hopes that the people who love your tips will flock to your website and buy your ingenious toy boxes, organizers, and bins.

The key to a good Tips Booklet is that it has great tips—high quality content. If you give readers great information that they can use, and it changes how they do things, they'll love you, trust your company, and buy your products.

Chapter 91. Who Cares about My Tips and How Does that Translate into Sales?

You'd be amazed at how much I don't know about automotive repair.

I'm a complete idiot about transmissions and valves and pings and shock absorbers. I don't know a spark plug from a carburetor—okay, maybe I do, but you get the idea: cars are not in my area of Nexpertise.

So, you can bet I'd love to get my hands on a Tips Booklet that gives me *The Top 25 Things You Need to Know so You Don't Get Ripped Off When You Take Your Car in for a Repair.*

Even now as I write this, I wonder, "Why have none of my local garages written a similar booklet?"

A Tips Booklet on this subject would be a sure-fire way to get my business. Why? Because if a garage owner is telling me how to look out for the signs that I'm being taken advantage of, then in my mind, he probably won't take advantage of me.

How's that for establishing trust right out of the gate?

And this is how it translates into sales: I would leave my old garage, where I'm unsure of fair pricing (because there is no way for me to know, since I know nothing about cars), and bring my car in to the new garage because I want to save money and I think the management will be—at the very least—fair and honest.

Guess what sound that garage owner is hearing?

Ka-ching!

And you can get this kind of customer/client loyalty, the kind that translates into some *ka-chings* for you too, by committing one weekend to creating a Tips Booklet that can be easily produced for the measly cost of your time, paper, and printing (at home or at a local Kinko's).

Fantastic, isn't it? I wish I had invented it!

Chapter 92. Don't Skimp on the Tips!

The success of your booklet is going to be based solely on the content.

You need to create a list in your Tips Booklet that is relevant to your audience. Again you need to remind yourself who they are, and create a list that speaks to what they need.

If my garage were trying to bring in new customers who have just moved into the neighborhood, the Tips Booklet would be perfect because when people move in they don't know the landscape. By positioning yourself as a loyal, honest, neighborhood garage, you are going to attract those people.

Great! But what if the garage wants to attract rich summer tourists who collect high-end cars? These folks know a thing or two about how an engine runs and they know a great deal about their cars, so they would be less concerned about fraud and more concerned about the garage's expertise in working with classic cars.

A booklet titled *25 Things You Absolutely Must Know About Maintaining Your Classic Car* might be better suited to this audience. This is a tempting booklet for car collectors because they love their vehicles and want to do everything they can to keep their cars in tip-top condition. The message is that the garage personnel understand their needs and, by extension, how to work on their cars.

So, you must craft a great title and a list of really wonderful ideas for the audience. The title should hook the reader and the tips should be thoughtful, unique, and inspired. They should answer a problem the reader might have.

Let's try to nail one down. First, let's think about your niche audience again. Sorry to be redundant, but you have to keep your target audience in mind every time you take on one of these communication/marketing projects—articles, speeches, booklets—because if you don't know who they are, you certainly can't address their needs.

So, remind yourself. Who is your niche audience again? (Remember, you can do different booklets for different audiences covering different interests. That garage might have two Tips Booklets—one for summer tourists and the other for year-round residents.)

For now, choose one niche audience:

_____

_____

_____

Now, let's think of some great list titles that might interest this group. Think of a list of 10, 25, or 50 ways to fix their problems, meet their needs, or provoke their interest. Have a couple of these? Even better. Write them down, and if you don't use them for the first booklet, you'll have fodder for the next. Start with these to get the juices flowing:

"25 Ways to…"

_____

_____

"10 Steps to…"

_____

_____

_____

"50 Ideas to…"

_____

_____

_____

"The Top 10 Strategies for…"

_____

_____

_____

"The 30 Most Popular Techniques for..."

_____

_____

_____

"How to Make the Most of Your..."

_____

_____

_____

Chapter 93. What Should I Write About?

You now have some ideas for catchy titles that will get people interested and maybe solve some of their problems.

Great!

Now you have to write the actual tips, and they have to be relevant and inspired!

Yikes!

It sounds like a tall order, but remember you are a Nexpert! You do this stuff every day. People pay you money to know what you know. You have years—maybe even decades—of experience. Once you get rolling, you'll be writing so fast you'll barely be able to keep up with your thoughts.

If you are a tax attorney specializing in working with homebased business owners, then maybe you've decided on a title like this one: *50 Things You Can Do to Prevent the IRS from Auditing Your Homebased Business*.

Whew!

That's a great title because what small business owner doesn't want to stay out of the spotlight of the IRS, right?

Now you are staring at the blank page thinking, "Great title—What do I write?"

You have to come up with some great tips. First do some research to get the ideas flowing. Go to the web, read some blogs, look up some info in your books, and jot down some notes whenever you see a relevant point—a myth that business owners mistakenly cling to, or some new rule from the IRS. Just get it on paper.

That is the key to brainstorming—Just getting information together and piling it onto the page. It doesn't have to be written perfectly. Your grammar can be off. You might even write down a bunch of ideas that will never make it into your booklet. Some stuff might not even make sense to you later. Or it might be better suited for another booklet.

Whatever.

The point behind brainstorming is that you get the ideas out there. Later you can organize them.

Do that now—just start doing your research. Write as much information as you can on a piece of paper. Don't edit yourself. Just get the ideas in front of you.

Go!

Chapter 94. Just Write It!

The great thing about making a list is that it isn't at all like writing a chapter book.

You don't have to have a long narrative or large blocks of text. You don't even need to organize and outline your ideas before you start. Because you can move things around, re-order the list, and add things you forgot, you can continually change and add without much confusion or grief.

You have all your ideas from your brainstorming list. Now, it's time to write:

1. **Put the title up first at the top of the page.** That will help you remember your message. Remember, every tip has to support your title. Your title is the whole point, the message, of the booklet.
2. **Check your brainstorming notes.** This ensures that you never have to come up with ideas while staring at the blank page. Start with the strongest points first, and start writing them one at a time. Don't worry about how many there are or whether they are articulated properly. Just get them on the page.
3. **As you write, you will probably think of new tips.** Writing does that. Just create a new number and add it. If you aren't sure you are going to keep an idea, leave it in and you can always delete later. Sometimes it's hard to know if one idea works until you see the whole thing in front of you. You can always go back later and re-jigger.

4. **Now that you have all your ideas out, leave it.** Walk away. Have a glass of wine in the backyard, or play a little ball with your twins. You will do better if you've cleared out the cobwebs. You'll probably find that new ideas will pop into your head while your mind is at rest. Take a notepad with you and make notes, if you want.

5. **When you come back rested and fresh, take a look at the list.** Start paring it down, adding new things, rearranging. Keep at it until you have a decent draft that you can work with. Go to bed, and you can get back at it the next day.

6. **Now, more of the same.** Put on the finishing touches, make the sentences sound great, check your grammar and punctuation—Oh! A word about this—no matter how smart or talented you are, if your booklet is filled with spelling, grammar, and punctuation mistakes, the reader will think you are a moron. Even a couple of little errors can send the message that you are careless and not good with details. If you aren't sure, ask someone who knows. And check and double check. And check it again.

7. **Give the draft to someone you trust—someone who will tell you the truth.** Ask them to look it over and be tough. Tough is the only thing that will help you. Then take their comments and go back and make corrections.

8. **Now you have a draft.** Put it away and start working on the look of your booklet.

Chapter 95. Remember—This Is a Project for a Long Weekend. Keep It Simple.

There are some booklet gurus out there who think you absolutely must hire a graphic designer to lay out the text and manage your logo.

I think it's a personal choice and I can live with either. You know your strengths. Do what's best for your business.

The choices are:

Go with a designer...

Have a designer go over your layout, if you don't mind that the booklet will take a little more time (lots of shuffling the drafts back and forth, waiting on the designer and negotiating the minutiae) and you'll have to shell out more money. The upside to this is that the layout will probably look more stylish and professionally done (you hope).

Or, go it alone.

The upside is that you forgo the costs of hiring someone and you really can nail this booklet in a weekend because there are fewer moving parts to manage. The downside is that you need to have a decent eye for design to get the layout looking good.

If you go the do-it-yourself route, here are some things to keep in mind:

- Keep it simple and go with clean lines.
- Keep the font basic—nothing ornate or scripted. Choose a font that is eye pleasing, and really, don't use five different fonts and sizes. Stick to one and go with it.
- Words do not need to be capitalized, bolded, *and* underlined—pick one and use it sparingly. These effects go a long way.
- Make sure you have lots of white space. Remember the stuff we discussed earlier in the book? Lists are great for white space. The eye loves to read a list because the page has so much white. If you can put a space in between each tip so that the page has more white, so much the better.
- Get rid of the clutter. I find clip art can be more distracting than useful. If you want to put a butterfly in the corner, great, but put *one* in, not eight.
- Use regular bullets. Those smiley face bullets are really distracting and just take away from your point.
- Make sure your contact info is easy to find and easy to read, and your company logo is placed in a visible area. Your name and/or company name should be on the cover under the title as well as inside the booklet or on the back cover. Don't use Tips Booklets with old information in them. It sends a message that you are not on top of your game.

Chapter 96. It's Easy to Become a Published Nexpert!

As if being published in a trade magazine or newspaper wasn't exciting enough!

Now you're about to publish your first Nexpert Tips Booklet.

Here's how:

Step 1: Lay out your final draft, your company logo and your contact information in the 4" x 9" size format. (This step may take a little longer if you use a designer.) If you are doing it yourself, keep it simple and do everything in a Word document.

Step 2: Download it onto a CD and bring it to Kinko's or e-mail it to them. Most copy shops will let you e-mail them a document if you call them first and find out what account to send it to.

Step 3: The nice folks at the copy shop will show you different bindings and different prices. Choose one and let them do their job.

Step 4: Go home with your box of professionally printed and bound booklets, and upload—or have your web guy upload—the booklet onto your website.

Wow! It's that easy to be a published Nexpert, and you didn't even need an editor or agent to do it!

Five Writing Tips for Your Tips

1. Keep each tip short, clear, and easy to read. You don't want one tip to be 10 sentences long and another super short. Keep them all about the same length. It will look better and more uniform.
2. Use short sentences to avoid punctuation and grammar problems.
3. Get rid of the jargon and speak to the masses.
4. Start each tip with an action word. Something like, "Organize your socks before you put them in the laundry—that will save you time later." Notice the word organize—a verb in the present tense—calls for people to do something. Another example is, "Create a new goal sheet every month that will help you keep losing weight." There are hundreds of action words and every tip should start with one. Some more are: assist, arrange, design, manage, fix, write, draw, assemble, motivate, challenge, etc.
5. Be specific. Sometimes people get convoluted when they write even though they normally are very articulate. If something sounds very complex and clunky, ask yourself, "What am I really trying to say here?" Then explain it out loud (or in your head) as if you were talking to someone. Then write whatever comes out of your mouth. It will probably be much clearer.

Chapter 97. Okay, I'm Lazy. Can I Just Create a Tips Sheet?

Yes. For you time-starved entrepreneurs out there, a tips sheet will work just fine (although the perceived value is not as high as for a Tips Booklet).

This is also a great alternative for the entrepreneur who wants to simplify the already simple process even more. The tips sheet allows you to forgo the whole copying/binding experience and lets you print them right on your home printer/copier.

No fuss. No muss. Even my mother could do this, and it costs pennies rather than dollars.

Tips sheets are generally printed on one or both sides of standard 8½" x 11" paper. The writing and look of the sheet is the same as it was for the booklet: Keep it clean and simple, use well-written list items, get rid of the butterflies, and make sure you include your contact information on both sides if you are writing on both sides.

One addition to this is the color of the paper. Tips sheets seem to be read more if they are done on a light colored paper: light green, blue, or pink. I'm not exactly sure why, but I think the color makes them stand out and seem special.

You can give your tips sheets out to the audience as a free marketing tool after you've spoken (or use them as barter to get business cards), and you can sell them on your website for a buck or two.

The sheets are a great alternative for people who really like to keep things simple. The process is much easier when you remove the printing/binding stage. But they are especially great for people who like to change their material a lot or work in a fast-changing business.

The process is so easy, you can potentially build a catalog of tip sheets that cover hundreds of topics. They can be printed as you need them or altered quickly for different audiences. Also, the tips can become ideas for columns, articles, speeches, and maybe even a book down the road.

The possibilities are endless.

Sell It or Give It Away?

It's a bit of a toss up, really.

On the one hand, this is a great freebie for your marketing campaign. On the other, it is an opportunity to open up another revenue stream.

If you sell your Tips Booklet, you can sell it to one customer at a time or in bulk to a single customer. There are arguments for both. The bulk method will get you more money up front than the piddling one-sale-at-a-time method on your website.

You can set the price based on the length, proprietary content, and comprehensiveness of the booklet, and whether your bulk buyer will require you to customize the booklet. In this scenario, you should weigh the bulk sale discount against the amount of work that goes into making changes for the buyer.

But if you go the one-at-a-time method, you may give up some quick upfront cash, but every time you sell or give away a booklet and capture each person's e-mail and/or mailing address, you add new people to your mailing list.

These people are potential customers for your other products and services. You don't get this with selling bulk because if you sell 1,000 booklets to one group, you have no idea to whom they gave the booklets, so although you have upfront money, you've lost a great opportunity to add a lot of new potential customers to your list.

If you use the booklet as a marketing tool, be generous. Give it away and feel good that you are getting your good name out there with a great message. The booklet will speak for you and give customers the time to think through how to use your services.

Don't skimp on the tips.

Many people are hesitant to give out too much information, especially if it's for free. The common thinking is, "If I tell them this, why will they want my other products and services?" But the opposite is usually the case.

People will think, "Wow! I got all this great information for free (or for only $7.95). Imagine all the stuff he's going to tell me in his $47 e-book (or his $197 seminar or whatever)!"

The point is, don't hold back in your booklet, speeches, or interviews. People will assume if that information is great, you have plenty more that's even better.

Chapter 98. Nifty Uses for My Tips Booklet

There are an infinite number of ways to use your Tips Booklet to help build your business. Here are a few ideas:

- Give them out as a free handout when you speak. You can leave them on the table and let people know they should come up and pick up the freebie, or even better, trade them for each participant's business card. This will help build up your mailing list and allow you to follow up with these potential clients.

- If you want to sell your booklet, know that you can sell them one at a time on your website, or for a bigger impact you can sell a bunch of them in bulk to a single buyer. For instance, the big gym in your town might be excited to buy 1,000 copies of your booklet, *20 Ways to Improve Your Life with Yoga*.

- Put the booklet in all your promotional kits and media packages. The booklets will show potential clients that you know how to market yourself and they'll respect you for it.

- Mail the booklet to people on your mailing list and include as a freebie for your direct mail campaign.

- Give customers the opportunity to go to your site and register for a free booklet if they sign up for a product or service. This is also a great way to build your e-mail list.

Will you give out your Tips Booklets at your speaking events or sell them on your website? Or both? Look over this list and pick two ways (those mentioned here or your own brilliant ideas) that your Tips Booklet can make you an even bigger Nexpert.

List them here:

1. _____

2. _____

Nexpert Story: Marie Genero

Marie Genero loved to give talks. She was great at it.

"I'm in my element on stage," she told me confidently. (I admit I was envious.)

Marie was a psychiatrist with her own homebased practice in Tampa, Florida. She worked for herself and often gave talks to companies in hopes of drumming up corporate work.

"My individual practice is thriving," she told me.

"But I put together this program that would help executives and workers handle stress better, and I wanted to test out my theories in the corporate world."

She was pretty sure her ideas could have an impact on worker productivity and a company's bottom line. Marie started doing seminars and attending business conferences in hopes of attracting new clients.

"The talks are going great," she told me over the phone.

"People love me. I'm handing out business cards like they're free iPods. I keep getting asked back."

But she was having trouble translating that success into paying clients.

"They love me in the room, but I never hear from them again. I can do two, three seminars a month and never get a call from it," she told me. "It's frustrating."

Marie's problem was that she had no setup and no follow-through. They forgot her as soon as she left the room.

"I didn't want to be sales-y. I'm a therapist and I have ethical responsibilities when I speak. I don't feel comfortable hustling. I just want to help people and have a healthy business."

We devised a pre- and post-talk strategy for her. It involved several components, but one of the most important ones was using a Tips Booklet as a marketing tool. It was perfect for Marie because a Tips Booklet could reinforce the good feelings people had for her talk. It would be, essentially, a reminder of how much they liked her and her ideas.

And because it provided tips that could really help people with no obligation, it didn't make her feel like she was selling.

continued

Marie wrote *30 Things You Can Do Today to Be Stress Free Tomorrow.* She told the audience that she would give them out for free with one caveat: "You have to work the tips and you have to give me your e-mail address so we can connect in a week and see how you're doing," she told them.

It worked because there was a next step after the speech. The connection wasn't over when her talk was over, and her influence carried into the real world.

"Because I had the booklet as a base, I felt comfortable talking to people and I made sure to give them easy, concrete things to do that would get real and immediate results. When they felt better at work, they knew I could do something for their department or company. Then, I could seal the deal."

The booklet, although a tiny little thing, can be a physical reminder of you; something that will help people remember you and remember how your message (and by extension, your services and products) can help them!

Chapter 99. Becoming a Nexpert Tips Booklet Author: Your Assignments for Days 62–66

Day 62: Remind yourself about your audience. Go to Chapter 92 and do the worksheet. Then pick the title for your booklet. There is an exercise in Chapter 92 to help you do that, too. If you go to Chapter 93, you will find some brainstorming strategies. Do the research and start brainstorming your tips. When you're done and your brain is fried, take a well-deserved break.

Day 63: Take a look at your brainstorming and organize your tips. Look at Chapter 94 for guidance. There are specific directions there to help you get through it. Get a good, substantial rough draft.

Day 64: Ask for feedback from trusted advisors. Finalize your draft. Lay out the text, contact info, and company logo. (You might need more time if you are using an outside designer.)

Day 65: Check the details, put the final product on a CD, and take it to a copy shop. Have them print out copies and bind them. Or print them and bind them yourself.

Day 66: In Chapter 98, I give you a bunch of different uses for the Tips Booklet. Finalize your strategy for how your Tips Booklet will help you, and fill in the exercise in that chapter.

Get crackin', Nexpert!

The Wrap-Up: Days 17–66

Become a Nexpert.

Day 17: Answer the question, "What does your business do?" in Chapter 62.

Day 18: Start talking like a Nexpert. When people ask you about your business, tell them what you've written above and repeat it until it feels natural.

Write Your Article and Get It Out to Publications.

Day 19: Define your niche audience. Complete the worksheet in Chapter 69. Buy some books about writing articles for magazines and newspapers.

Day 20: Research where these customers are getting their information from and complete the worksheet in Chapter 70.

Day 21: Research these publications. Find out what kind of stories are being written and are of interest to your audience.

Day 22: Read about writing.

Day 23: Brainstorm ideas for stories, start an idea file, and add ideas as you go along.

Days 24–26: Create a pitch for the article and begin to call editors.

Day 27: Call more editors and refine the pitch.

Day 28: Keep calling until someone likes your idea and wants to work with you.

Days 29–30: Create a one-page proposal of your article based on your conversation with the editor.

Day 31: Refine your proposal and send it to editor.

Days 32–38: Begin writing (or start looking for a ghostwriter). Call back editor(s).

Days 39–40: Ask for feedback. Take criticism. Make edits.

Day 41: Submit to editor.

Prepare Your Talk and Set Dates.

Day 42: Fill in the blanks in Chapters 82, 83, and 84. Decide who is your audience, what message you want to send, and what kind of speech you will prepare.

Days 43–44: Research the best speaking opportunities in your area. Look for organizations that are rich in your niche target audience and qualify as great speaking opportunities (use the criteria in Chapter 80). Contact the organizers.

Day 45: Outline your talk and create a short, one-page proposal outlining what you will speak about, how long the talk will be, and the format in which you will deliver the talk (workshop, seminar, formal speech, etc.)

Day 46: Gather the materials to send to the organizers. This will include a short bio for them to send to attendees, a picture, and any material that you feel helps position you as a Nexpert.

Days 47–49: Send out the proposal and information about you and your business by e-mail. Follow up with organizers after they receive your information. Call new ones and send them proposals. Be persistent; don't give up.

Days 50–56: Write and prepare for your talk. Keep talking to new and existing organizers. Set dates for talks and firm up details.

Day 57: Practice the talk in front of a mirror or camera. Critique yourself. Then give it to a practice audience or friend. Get feedback. Practice and work out the kinks.

Days 58–60: Rewrite and hone the speech. Practice giving the speech again to work out any final kinks, and have your practice audience throw questions at you for the Q&A session. Finalize speaking dates and go over last-minute issues.

Day 61: Keep going over the speech every few days until you speak. When the time comes, enjoy that you finally got what you deserve—you are a Nexpert Speaker!

Write Your Tips Booklet.

Day 62: Remind yourself about your audience. Go to Chapter 92 and do the worksheet. Then pick the title for your booklet. There is an exercise in Chapter 92 to help you do that. If you go to Chapter 93, you will find some brainstorming strategies. Do the research and start brainstorming your tips. When you're done and your brain is fried, take a well-deserved break.

Day 63: Take a look at your brainstorming and start to organize your tips. Look at Chapter 94 for guidance. There are specific directions there to help you get through it. Get a good substantial rough draft.

Day 64: Ask for feedback from trusted advisors. Finalize your draft. Lay out the text, contact info, and company logo. (You might need more time if you are using an outside designer.)

Day 65: Check the details, put the final product on a CD, and take it to a copy shop. Have them print out copies and bind them. Or print them and bind them yourself.

Day 66: In Chapter 98, I give you a bunch of different uses for the Tips Booklet. Finalize your strategy for how your Tips Booklet will help you, and fill in the exercise in that chapter.

Keep going! Look what you are accomplishing!

WRAP-UP

Part

How to Be a Nexpert 102

Taking Your Newfound Nexpertise
To the Next Level

"A real entrepreneur is somebody who has no safety net underneath them."

—*Henry Kravis*

Media Interviews:
Send Out a Press Release and
Set Up Two Interviews with the Press

"Do one thing every day that scares you."

—*Eleanor Roosevelt*

Chapter 100. I'm on a Roll, Jeff—What's Next?

If you've been following along in this book, then you can pat yourself on the back.

You are doing a lot to grow your business. And you are doing it quickly. You should see your confidence as a Nexpert growing, and you should start seeing your visibility increasing in your niche even at this early stage. Keep this up and you should see a real change in your bottom line and your lifestyle.

If you haven't yet, keep moving forward. It'll happen. This is the work of good marketing. And good marketing—getting the word out on the street about you—will always help your business.

What I want you to do now is—as Emeril Lagasse says—"Kick it up a notch!"

I want you to take your Nexpertise to the next level. It's great that you've given a couple of good talks. (You have, haven't you?) You've crafted an article and created a Tips Booklet to use as a marketing tool. Mix that with your stellar products and services and you now have something to talk about.

It's time to talk to the press.

I want you to use the media in your area—mainly print and radio to start—to your advantage, to help you get closer and more intimate with your niche.

This can be daunting. It was scary enough to go out on stage and wear the cloak of the Nexpert. It will be intimidating to talk to a seasoned journalist who may also know your niche well.

But remember: you are the Nexpert. You deserve to be there.

Why? Because that's how you've positioned yourself. That's your public persona.

Embrace it and make it work for you!

Chapter 101. If You Scratch Your Nose, Call a Journalist

It isn't enough to do great things or have great products and services.

You have to tell people about it. And you have to keep telling them. You have to make a habit of telling your niche what you are doing, and a good way to do that is to keep the press interested in you and your business.

Journalists are always looking for good stories to tell. It is their job to come up with great content to fill their newspapers and airtime. They are hungry for a good story. Your job is to deliver it right into their hands.

Every time you do something—get a new client, give a talk, write an article, create a new product, provide a new service—you need to talk to the press about it. It needs to be part of your ongoing communications plan.

You need to do it until it becomes natural.

Get a new gig. Call the press. Give a new talk. Call the press. Develop a great new system to make something easier for your clients. Call the press. Scratch your nose. Call the press. This needs to be a regular communication tool for your business. It is another way for you to continually talk to your niche audience.

Remember, though, that journalists are not at all like your customers and colleagues. They are—excuse the generalization—quite jaded as a group. And for good reason.

They've seen every pitch out there. They're juggling lots of persistent PR people desperate to get their clients in the media. And they've already written a couple thousand stories of their own.

They are not easily impressed.

So your story needs to be compelling and interesting. It needs to have an angle that grabs the reader. It must be unique.

It's a tall order, but you can do it. You're a Nexpert, and you want the people in your niche to know that and get the message consistently.

Say Yes—Then Jump!

My friend Alex produces rock concerts and special events. He has an in-triguing philosophy that drives his business. He says, "Say yes, and then try to make it happen."

He makes a commitment to seize an opportunity and then he goes for it.

Why is this an important life strategy? Because if an opportunity comes up and you don't grab it immediately, your brain will start to play games with you.

It will ask, "Can I do this?"

"Am I capable?"

"Do I deserve this?"

It will come up with a million reasons why you should play it safe. It will talk you out of taking a risk. It will remind you that you can't possibly do it!

The way to prevent your brain from taking over is to do what Alex does. He believes that if you commit, it forces you to make it work. It gives you added incentive.

"You can't turn tail and run or duck out when no one is looking," Alex says.

When an opportunity comes up, say, "Yes!" Don't think about it. Don't waiver. Just commit. Then figure out how to make it happen. Live up to the new challenge. You have to storm ahead when you don't have a way to wiggle out.

If it doesn't work out, you can lick your wounds and do your mea culpa. You have little to lose, and much to gain.

That's how you grow a business!

Chapter 102. Get Yourself an Interesting Angle

I mentioned back in Chapter 3 that every year I sponsor something called The Home Office From Hell Contest.

I ask homebased entrepreneurs from around the country to write me and tell me about their own personal home offices from hell. The winner of the contest always has a horrific home office situation and is able to talk about it with some wit and self-deprecation. There are so many incredible stories that it's often quite difficult to choose a winner.

Homebased business owners are a savvy, ingenious group—even when all is not going well—and their responses are always both enlightening and hilariously poignant. My wife Barbara and I love reading the entries. There is nothing quite like curling up on the couch together and laughing riotously over the stories, each one better than the last. They are witty, savvy, and creative. I have no worries that this group can get out of their caves and become Nexperts.

The contest helped me see that creativity. It helped me get to know my niche. It helped me identify problems that homebased business owners were having, and it inspired me to create solutions for them. Reading these entries inspired me to write this book.

But these were unexpected upsides.

The contest started purely as a way to get my business in the media.

I needed a hook to get journalists to want to write about me. So I thought up the contest and made it happen. And sure enough, the journalists bit.

Stories about the contest have appeared in more than 1,000 media outlets including TV, radio, newspapers, magazines, Internet websites, and blogs. Our story was picked up by the Associated Press, Scripps-Howard, and other news wire services, CNN Headline News, Inc.com, *Costco Magazine*, and hundreds of local newspapers and other publications around the country.

You don't necessarily have to create a contest, but you do need a unique, attention-grabbing angle.

So, let's get you one!

Chapter 103. Developing Your Angle

In this chapter, I'm going to help you find a great angle for your story.

This is where you need to think creatively. You need to consider your niche customers and what they would like to read.

Your goal is to inform and entertain them. (Remember? We discussed tone and intention in Chapter 84.) You should be knowledgeable and interesting. Your ideas should help them learn something about how to improve their lives or their business, but not preach or talk down to them. Your hook should turn a dry idea into something provocative, controversial, funny, quirky, or interesting.

That's how you will further your Nexpertise with your niche.

Here are some ideas to get you started thinking about different angles:

- **Create a contest.** A contest always attracts the press. It gives them lots of angles to work with: the contest itself, the prizes, the entrepreneur hosting it, and the quirky contestants.

- **Solve a problem.** Is every resident in your town up in arms about the gophers tearing up the lawns? Well, if you can offer them a few solutions, you can definitely get the press' attention. Think about the problems of your niche audience and come up with some timely solutions.

- **Make a discovery.** Did you discover the key to taking off baby weight? How about a technology that can help people get through their e-mails more quickly and cut two hours out of their workday? If you've got a discovery—particularly a good one—it could attract significant buzz.

- **Get an award or nomination.** It doesn't matter if it is the Golden Nose or the Golden Globes; no one really knows how prestigious an industry award is (barring maybe the Oscars). So get some press about it!

- **Host an event.** Are you teaching a seminar? Hosting a dinner for luminaries in your field? Are you hosting a dance marathon for charity? Tell the press. It's a fun way to get a mention!

- **Make a prediction.** Do you think you can forecast the economy or the next presidential election? If you're right, you can publicize it. If not, you can talk about the surprising things that happened to change the predicted outcome. "He was primed to win the election, until he ran out of money and his campaign was derailed. Who could've seen that coming?"

- **Have interesting or quirky clients.** Are you proud of the dress you made for the local girl who is getting married next week? Maybe you can convince a journalist to cover the wedding for the Sunday Styles section, and get a sidebar about your work on the dress.

- **Be a philanthropist.** Do you and your employees run the 20-mile run for breast cancer every year? If so, don't be afraid to see if the press wants to interview you and talk about your passion for the cause. It's good for your business and for the charity.

- **Overcome challenges.** Do you have a VA who battles MS and still makes your business run smoothly? Maybe she would be a great subject for a piece on extraordinary people who overcome big challenges. Did you battle back from bankruptcy only to break a million this year? That is fodder for a great rags-to-riches story. People love to read these inspirational pieces.

- **Be a hometown boy/girl who makes good.** These stories are easy to place. Every local paper is looking for a story about a hometown boy or girl who goes out into the world, slays the lions, and lives to tell the tale. A friend of mine who was recently nominated for a Tony Award for his Broadway musical had his local hometown papers write several stories about him. One journalist even spent the day with his mother for the piece.
- **Go green (or whatever your cause).** Environmental causes are huge right now. If you pride yourself on being a green company, pitch yourself to the press and talk about what you and your staff do to be green. This applies to every other hot cause *du jour*.
- **Have a great corporate culture.** Do you and your employees meditate together? Go on rock climbing expeditions once a month? Do you have hardly any turnover and want to share the secrets of keeping employees happy and productive? This might be a great business section article.
- **Be the contrarian.** When everyone says "sell," you say "buy." When they say, "It's blue," you say, "No way, it's red!" If you're always playing the devil's advocate, this might be a great angle for you. Taking a contrarian opinion sets you apart and makes you different; Bill O'Reilly and Al Franken have built media careers on doing just that. Don't be afraid to be different. Don't shy away from controversy; it's your friend. People will remember you—even if they dislike your position!
- **Become an advocate.** Be a part of social issues that relate to your business. Maybe you make products for children and you hear that a child at a local park was hurt by some unsafe conditions there. This is an opportunity to perhaps make a donation of some of your products, and go on a media crusade about the importance of safe equipment for children.

You get the idea. The way you can create an angle is only limited by your imagination. Now it's your turn.

I want you to write down three story angles that you might want to pitch to the press. Each angle should be no more than a couple of sentences. Keep it concise, clear, and specific. Be creative. Think about your niche audience: Who are they? What would they like to read? What are they listening to?

After you've got three potential stories, look them over carefully. Think about what will pique your audience's interest the most and get them interested in you. Think—what story angle will best highlight your Nexpertise and grow your business?

Then, go with the strongest idea. That will be the basis for your pitch.

Story Angle #1
I want to pitch a story about...

_____

_____

_____

_____

Story Angle #2
I want to pitch a story about...

_____

_____

_____

_____

Story Angle #3
I want to pitch a story about...

_____

_____

_____

_____

Chapter 104. Ten Steps to the Perfect Pitch

You have your story idea, but that is only the beginning.

You can't go to a reporter or the producer of a talk radio show with a vague idea about a great story:

"I think, um … I might want to, you know, write…uh…something about deer and how they might be … kinda overpopulated … or something … in our area … don't ya think?"

You have to go to the press with a fully fleshed-out angle and story. You have to do their work for them and hand it to them on a silver platter. Take that well-written two-sentence angle and make it into a full-fledged story.

How do you do that?

Well, let's work it through together. I've broken the brainstorming and outlining process into 10 easy steps. Work them and create a great pitch!

Let's pretend we wrote the following as our story angle in the last chapter:

I can show do-it-yourselfers how to put in their own copper eyebrows (on the roofs of their houses). It will improve the look and value of their home and they can do it themselves in a weekend without hiring a contractor.

This is a valuable tip for a niche audience. If you are interested in doing your own renovations and repairs, you'll be excited to read this piece.

Step 1. Keep this simple angle at the top of your page. This is your message and your inspiration. If you get off track, just keep going back to the message.

Step 2. Now that you have the basis for a pitch, think about to whom you will pitch it. Do you want to pursue newspapers, websites, bloggers, columnists, radio, TV? Are you thinking about getting a radio interview on the Saturday home improvement show on your local radio station? Or is this more of an article for the Home section of the local paper?

Think locally, because you will have more success and be able to hit your niche audience head on. Consider your dream article: what media outlet will best get you some talk time with your niche audience? What outlet will be best for growing your business?

Try for different kinds of media—I suggest radio and print (and that's what we'll cover in this section)—these are great ways to get your feet wet and you can almost always be interviewed by telephone from the comfort of your home or office.

Step 3. Okay, so go ahead. Choose five media outlets that reach your audience and might help you ramp up your Nexpertise. Be specific about your goals. Don't just write "newspaper." Write *The Nickelsaver* or *The Pulp City Times-Union* or "Dick Sturgeon's Business Hour on WKLJ."

The five media outlets I'll be pitching are:

1. _____

2. _____

3. _____

4. _____

5. _____

Now that you know what outlets you'll be pitching to, you'll need to find the right reporter, producer, or editor to hear your pitch. If you are pitching your home improvement story, you don't want to pitch the automotive editor.

Step 4. Research the media outlets you've chosen. Do an article search. Find out which journalists have done articles on topics similar to your own. Make a list of those reporters and some of the articles they've written.

Step 5. Research your own topic. You have to have the specifics of this article fleshed out before you call the reporter. Look for facts and figures to boost your pitch:

"The manager of the local lumber store reports that there are some 2,000 people in town considered to be avid do-it-yourselfers—that is, people who do at-home renovations and projects at least six times a year."

These kinds of facts tell the reporter that there is an audience for her article.

Step 6. Think about your experience and why you would be a great subject for the article:

"The Fix-It Shop has asked me to do several seminars teaching people how to faux treat their walls and improve the exterior of their homes. I specialize in working with wrought iron and copper, and several of the houses in the new, upscale housing development feature my work."

Step 7. Don't forget any provocative tidbits that might make this an even better sell:

"I think people often feel taken advantage of by contractors. I want to inspire people to start these projects on their own, and feel good that they are improving the value of their homes while saving themselves money and headaches."

Step 8. Elaborate on this by saying, "I have five easy steps to help people get the job done in a single weekend." This kind of list of steps or tips is always great because it simplifies the process and makes it a skimmable, easy read for the audience.

Step 9. Know as much about your subject matter as possible. Then flesh out your pitch a bit more. You might want to start with something like this on the phone with the reporter:

"Hi Kathy, I read your piece on wrought iron railings and thought it was very helpful for do-it-yourselfers. I have a great story idea about how to install copper eyebrows on the roof without having to pay a contractor to have it done. I recently gave a seminar that helped two homeowners in town to do it themselves and they safely completed the job in a single weekend. I know that many of your readers are do-it-yourselfers, and I think this piece might be a great way for them to dress up their house without having to call in the cavalry."

This is a great way to begin.

Notice that in this pitch, I implied several important things: (a) I had read and liked her articles (proving that I had done my research), (b) I knew her audience and had a great story just for them, and (c) I was an expert in the field because I had taught a seminar on it.

This kind of pitch should get you in the door if the journalist is at all interested in the subject matter. This format also applies when you are pitching for radio and TV—you will be contacting the producer of the show. (The producer might be the on-air personality or he might not, so check it out first.) Either way, that person may ask you to write this all down and send it in a pitch letter. This is a good sign.

Follow the steps outlined above and put your phone pitch down on paper. Keep it to one page only. The pitch letter will give the reporter some time and space to consider your idea more thoroughly.

Step 10. Keep honing your pitch and keep calling reporters. Be concise, unique, and assertive. This is how you set your company apart from the others!

Chapter 105. Pitching to the Press

Now that you have your great story angle, I want you to take that story to the press. Get them to sit up and notice you. Here are some tips to make a great pitch:

- **Know your journalist.** Who is this journalist? What does she write about? If she writes about technology, she will not be able to do anything with your pitch about your knitting business. You will have wasted her time and yours.
- **Don't make the journalist work too hard.** Come to the table with a completed story: Don't tell the journalist you were thinking of a story about how the pet food industry is probably reeling from the recent food poisoning scandal—with no idea if it really is. That leaves the journalist to do all the legwork, and I'm gonna tell you—they probably won't do it. The burden is on you to flesh out a complete story. Instead, pitch a story about how the pet food store you own has been impacted by the scare and what you are doing to calm customers' fears and protect their pets from harm.
- **Call and leave a message.** Journalists are very busy and often they are not at their desks. These are great opportunities to leave short pitches on their answering machines. Be quick. Give them the important points, explain why your story is interesting to the reader, and leave your number. Don't drone on, explaining all the intricacies. Just get in and get out. They'll appreciate you for it.
- **Be flexible.** If the journalist is open to your idea but wants to take it in another direction, be flexible. They know more about what their readers want than you do.
- **Make yourself available.** If a journalist is interested, make their job easy. Give them lengthy interviews or access to anything that will make the story better: colleagues, family, employees, and non-confidential papers. Do whatever will help them get to know you and build a better article. Don't forget that journalists are always on deadline, so if they contact you for a story and need to speak with you by a certain time on a certain day, drop everything you are doing and make yourself available. Make sure they have your cell phone number so they can reach you wherever/whenever. They don't care about your other important call, your dental appointment, or your kid's soccer game. Help them out and they'll be back again for more. Screw them up and you can forget about ever dealing with them again.
- **Say thanks.** Always follow up with a nice note or e-mail saying thanks. And don't be afraid to keep in touch. That reporter should be a contact for life.

Chapter 106. Talking to the Press with Your Press Release

Some entrepreneurs prefer to pitch and others prefer to send press releases. Some do both. Press releases are a great way to keep reporters and your public informed.

Once you create a compelling story angle and write out the details supporting the story in your release, that single page can go out to dozens or thousands of media outlets. Even better, you can choose exactly where you want it to go. So if you only want to have your release go to food journalists in Kansas City, you can target that audience.

News wire services, like PR Newswire, can send your press release out nationally (for a hefty fee) or to your local papers and radio stations for an affordable fee. If you have only a few specific journalists you want to target, you can forgo the whole news wire expense and just send your press release directly to those journalists.

Whatever manner you prefer, the press release is a great way to write down your pitch once and have that single piece of paper sent to lots of people. If you are uncomfortable with phone pitching, this might be a more comfortable alternative for you. Some entrepreneurs like to send the release first and then follow up with a phone call. That way they can begin the conversation like this:

"Hi Joe! I just sent over a press release this morning about the new talk I'm doing in two weeks."

Joe: "Hi, yes, I received it."

"You might recall I'm planning on giving away my booklet, *30 Ways that Colonics Can Change Your Life,* and I thought your readers might be interested in that!"

(A conversation is started.)

The press release cuts out that anxiety-ridden ten seconds where you are trying to tell Joe your exciting idea and he may be distracted or right in the middle of something else.

Another plus is that press releases aren't just for the eyes of journalists anymore. You can release your press release online through one of the services like PR Newswire and it will be posted and archived by search engines such as Google and Yahoo. That means your niche audience can find your press release by doing a regular key word search. You can have an ongoing conversation with your target audience and never actually speak to a journalist. This is great news for the pitch-challenged!

And here's another interesting thing. Journalists use the search engines to gather facts and information about the articles they are writing; if they see your name and company name often enough, they may contact you without your even having to contact them.

Imagine that, no pitch letters! They just might start chasing you!

Chapter 107. Anatomy of a Press Release

There is a specific formula for writing a press release, but once you get it, it's in your brain forever.

If you are one of the two people on earth who has never seen a press release, go to the Internet and print one out. There are millions out there. Many are in the company communications folder on any business website. Having one in your hand will help you get a visual to use as inspiration.

Here is the basic structure of a press release:

FOR IMMEDIATE RELEASE:
This is usually placed in the upper left margin. It is always capitalized.

A Compelling Headline: State your exciting news. Use specifics and make it sound sensational. Try this:

> Legendary Horse Racing Trainer, Kip Staler, wins coveted NHRA
> Lifetime Achievement Award in his hometown of Saratoga Springs,
> New York.

This is exciting, has lots of specifics, and gives reporters a couple of different angles: horse racing, hometown boy makes good, Saratoga lifestyles, etc.

Dateline: The city and the release is sent from, and the date.
    Saratoga Springs, New York, June 12, 2008

Lead Paragraph: This is the angle of your story. The first sentence of the release should be very strong and hook the reader. It will contain the information that is most essential to the message. It includes the five Ws: who, what, where, when, and why. Here's an example:

> The National Horse Racing Association honored longtime Saratoga resident and top-rated horse trainer Kip Staler Saturday night with their highest honor, The Lifetime Achievement Award, and hosted a gala benefit at the Casino in the Park, with a star-studded audience in attendance.

If you are writing this press release with the intention of having it archived by Google and other search engines, try to get as many good keywords in the lead paragraph and headline without messing up the content and style of your writing.

The Body: This is where you write out the details of your message. In this case, who attended the gala, details of what was served, quotes from the guests, quotes from the award winner, information about the award, etc. You should assemble the information from most important first to least important last. For instance, if it is important to you that the reader knows how prestigious the honor is, that information should be placed in the first paragraph, and details about the menu should be included in the last.

Company Boilerplate: End with a short bio about yourself and your company. In these few lines (three to five tops) you can refer to your products, services, and a short company history. Be concise. The news in the press release will sell you, not your bio!

Contact Information: Don't forget this one! Include your name, company name, website address, phone, and e-mail address.

Chapter 108. Yikes! The Reporters Bit. I Have Interviews Coming Up!

This is what you wanted!

Now, you're going to have an opportunity to talk to the press and send your message out to your core audience. This is going to help your business and really help you seal your Nexpert status!

In the following sections, we're going to prepare you for your interviews. I will give you some tips for print and radio.

Be excited that you are taking risks. You really are a maverick. This is what it's all about. This is how you make your business better. It's how you make your life better.

Chapter 109. The Radio Talk Show

Radio interviews are a great way to get your foot in the door with the press.

There are hundreds of radio talk shows out there and they are looking for great content, just like any media outlet. Make sure you target shows that speak to your niche audience. You want them listening when you dazzle them with your charisma and great ideas!

Try to get your interview aired during drive time; that's Monday through Friday from about 6 A.M. to 9 A.M., and then from 5 P.M. until around 6:30 P.M. So, what's the best time? Probably 7:30 A.M. to 8:30 A.M., with around 7:30 A.M. being the best. Why? That's peak rush hour when everyone is stuck in traffic!

The best days of the week are probably Tuesday and Wednesday. Try to avoid Fridays; many people take off or are thinking about the weekend. Mondays are better than Friday, but many people are still trying to recover from the weekend!

Contact the show's producer or on-air personality and pitch them your story angle. If they bite, they'll schedule you to do either a taped or live interview.

You can also put an ad in Radio Television Interview Report (www.rtir.com). This could get you national coverage. This publication has a subscription base of some 5,000 TV and radio producers. Turns out many of these producers are looking for content for their shows, and this is a great way to get their attention.

Stay local to hit your niche audience, but if you have a national business, remember that you need to hit the big markets. Pay no attention to rankings and claims about market dominance; a salsa station in New York is in the #1 market but your niche might not be there. Find out the actual number of listeners. You won't make much of a dent if you are doing 50 interviews on tiny stations. Do fewer interviews with bigger audiences.

The big thing about radio is that you never have to set foot in the studio. Yes, you can be in your bathrobe with your hair in curlers and a green mud mask on your face, and still speak like an authority; no one will be the wiser!

Radio is a great opportunity to speak directly to your audience and do it all over the phone.

Chapter 110. Radio Tricks and Tips

Here's how to ace your radio interview:

- **Be prepared.** I suggest writing out a list of questions that interviewers will most likely ask (or you would like them to ask). Make notes on each question and keep them in front of you in case you lose your place. But don't read!
- **Know the program and the interviewer.** What is the interviewer's background? What stories is he into? Is he confrontational? Does he like to make people cry on air? Know whom you're dealing with before you start.
- **Send promotional materials and information before your interview.** If you have background and reading materials that help the interviewer get familiar with the story, offer to send it to the producer before the show. This also might include complementary copies of your Tips Booklet.
- **Be brief.** Your answers should not be long-winded, with superfluous details. After more than half a minute you are pushing the limit. This does not mean you should answer a curt "yes" or "no" whenever you are asked a question. It does mean you must find a middle ground. Be interesting, entertain, and inform listeners, but don't do a monologue.
- **Be charismatic and excited.** If you are passionate and excited about the topic, it will be contagious. Use colorful language, and your voice should not be monotone and flat. If you are funny, be funny, but stay away from jokes that can fall flat. The silence on the air will be deafening and it will be hard to recover the interview.
- **Be personal and intimate.** I don't want you to read your résumé on air, but a personal story that illustrates your message will help drive the point home and endear you to listeners. If you are answering questions from call-in listeners, remember their names and use them when you answer their questions. It makes people feel important and heard.

- **Repeat the question.** When the interviewer asks a question, restate it before you answer. This helps you be sure you understand the question, gives the interviewer a chance to rephrase if he needs to, and keeps you from blurting out a response that is less than thoughtful. A win-win all around!
- **Put a sign on the door to your office (or bedroom).** It should say, "I'm On The Radio—Do Not Enter!" Let everyone in the family or office know in advance that you are being interviewed, and tell them what you expect from them. You don't want to be making a fantastic point only to have your screaming toddler burst in and throw herself into your lap! Also, put the dog out if he's going to bark when the FedEx guy shows up!
- **Use a landline telephone.** Don't do your interview on a cell phone. A minute of bad reception will ruin your interview.
- **Be yourself.** Don't try to be funny if you're not. Don't try to talk about stuff that isn't in your area of expertise. Don't try to be casual and laid back if you are naturally uptight and formal. It will never work. It will feel forced and plastic. Or worse, it'll sound like you're trying too hard. Just be who you are—that's good enough!
- **Keep your eye on the clock.** If you know they've scheduled 15 minutes for the interview, start your wrap-up with 2 minutes to go. That way you won't be cut off in the middle of an incredible point!
- **Follow up.** Always follow up with a note about how much you enjoyed the interview. It is good form and will help them remember you well.

Nexpert Story: Bobby Hargrove

"I love radio interviews!" Bobby told me.

"I do a couple a month and it has really changed my business."

Bobby Hargrove is a beekeeper and honey producer in Madison, Wisconsin. On first look, you might think the radio is a strange place to market yourself as a beekeeper. I mean, how many honey bee fans are listening in on the radio right now?

But this is the beauty of the radio interview; it seems there is always a place for good content whether you are a buttoned-down accountant being interviewed on

continued

Nexpert Story: Bobby Hargrove

a serious financial talk show or a quirky entrepreneur with an oddball business.

According to Bobby, radio is a great place for getting publicity for your business, even if it doesn't seem like the perfect fit at first.

"People told me I was wasting my time when I first started doing radio interviews," he told me.

"No one thought the radio could help me sell honey or help me grow my business."

But Bobby had a boisterous, colorful personality that was a perfect fit for radio. He also had a gift for telling a story and a business that people found quirky and interesting. More importantly, he had a great angle:

"Every jar of my honey has a nice little saying on it. The little bits of wisdom are hokey and sentimental, but I put these on the jars with a bit of a nod and a wink—and people get that."

Bobby's radio interviews started with him telling some animated beekeeping-gone-wrong stories. Then the interviewer asked him about the sayings on the jars, how he thought them up, and how he decided which ones to put on the jars, etc.

It intrigued the audience and people started calling in to ask what the saying of the day was. The radio interviewer liked his taped interviews so much, he asked him to come on the air and do a live interview. Now Bobby does a segment a couple times a month where the host pretends to call him up out of the blue and see what the saying of the day is. "It's all contrived, but people know that and they seem to get a kick out of knowing we are trying to have some fun with them."

More importantly, Bobby's tongue-in-cheek persona has become quite popular with the locals and several outlying counties. He has gotten a lot of local media attention, and people recognize his honey because "it has the hokey sayings on the jar."

As a result, his honey sales have increased 22 percent over the last year. He has developed new products, such as honeycomb candles and honey products infused with lavender and herbs—each labeled with one of his famous sayings. These products have been well received.

continued

The secret to his success is twofold:

1. *Bobby knows his strengths. He can tell a folksy story, and knows he can use his big personality to his advantage on the radio.*
2. *He has a brilliant angle that he can use to get people to connect with him and his product.*

When you go on the radio, it doesn't matter whether you have an offbeat business and a big personality or a quiet demeanor and a more traditional company. Different show formats require different personalities and areas of expertise. There's a format out there that is perfect for you!

The point is, you need to focus on your strengths and go with what makes you special and unique. And you need to have a great, attention-getting angle that will get people to give you a second look—or in this case a second listen!

Chapter 111. Your Print Interview

It feels good when the phone rings and a journalist is on the other end eager to talk to you about your compelling story.

The main thing you want to do is be prepared. Good preparation is a great offense *and* defense. The better prepared you are, the more confident you'll sound—that will show through in your interview.

Here are some pointers to get you to an optimal level of confidence with the press:

- **Come to the table with something to say.** Keep your notes in front of you, with statistics and facts to back up your message and a reminder to tell that story that will drive home the point. If you have notes in front of you, it will help keep you on message and supply you with a handy reference if you draw a blank.
- **Be interesting and have timely ideas.** Be specific. Vague, obscure philosophizing will bore the reporter and might even give him the impression you are hiding

something. Be engaging and transparent. Tell the truth. Use concrete examples to back up your ideas. Go with ideas that you think will pique the journalist's interests.

■ **Be yourself.** Journalists are trained to be perceptive. If you try to be someone you're not, they'll sniff you out like a pig with a truffle. Just relax and don't be afraid to show them who you really are. Don't lie or falsify any information. It's just too easy today to Google something, and reporters are trained to investigate the facts.

■ **Let the interviewer lead.** Don't try to set the tone of the interview. The journalist will feel the shift and it might come off as manipulative. Worse, you don't want to turn the journalist against you. This is an opportunity to be heard. Let the reporter set the tone and do the interviewing.

■ **Speak slowly.** There is some research that suggests that people who speak more slowly send a message of power, confidence, and authority. We listen harder to people who speak more slowly. It also gives you some space to get your head around the answer if you need more time!

■ **Keep your eye on the message.** Keep your eye on the prize. Know what you want to get across before the interview, and try your best to communicate that message. Back it up with interesting points and a good story or two. Avoid being dragged into unimportant tangents.

■ **Know your journalist.** Get an idea ahead of time what he is looking for and give it to him. He is probably looking for some great quotes from you, a general understanding of the issues, and maybe one or two new tidbits that he can use to make his article sound new.

■ **Be easy.** That means be accessible and available. If you can give the journalist extra information, more time, put him in touch with another source, or anything that helps him write a better article, do it. This also means that if you say you're going to do something, you must do it. And don't waste his time by not being available when you say you will be.

Chapter 112. Four Things You Should Never Say in an Interview

"I'll tell you the dirt but it has to be off the record."

Don't assume you can say, "This is off the record," and it will be. There is no such thing. Watch what you say. You might like the reporter, but he is still writing a story about you. Maybe he'll respect it. Maybe not. In the end, he'll write what he wants to write.

"Am I prattling on?"

Reporters love people who talk incessantly. They sit back and let the awful quotes fall out of your mouth while they take copious notes. If you have a tendency to gab on endlessly and can often be heard *saying too much*, keep yourself in check. This is no time for verbal diarrhea.

"Let's meet for a drink."

Don't do interviews over drinks. It's okay for the media savvy, but amateurs and talkers should stay clear of anything that impairs their judgment.

"How could you write that?!" Expect the unexpected when you see your article for the first time. I've given long interviews and spent hours with reporters only to find that for all my trouble, I only got a small mention in a lengthy article. Or even worse, they mostly wrote about my competitors. It may smart for a day or so, but don't even think about calling the reporter and giving him an earfull.

Instead, call him and tell him you enjoyed the piece and liked working with him. Let him know you are available anytime and would be happy to be a source for him should he need a quote, other contacts in your industry, some research, or other information. This will position you well for the future when you pitch him again. You have no control over what the press will say in the article; they can misquote you, make you look silly, leave out your business partner's name, or take you completely out of context. And sooner or later it will happen. Just let it go and accept it as part of the deal.

Nexpert Story: Troy Heller

"All I know was that I was nervous and when I get nervous I talk a lot," Troy Heller told me.

Troy pitched a local reporter to do a publicity piece on him after he was nominated for a Best Business of the Year award by a Seattle, Washington small business organization. Troy's accounting company was being recognized for having some of the most progressive and employee-friendly programs in the city. *continued*

Nexpert Story: Troy Heller

"I was excited to do the piece. I hoped to win the award and I thought getting a few nice profiles in the local press would help us seal the deal," he told me.

"...and maybe help us pick up a few more clients."

Troy expected the reporter to ask him a few questions about his business practices and his innovative employee programs.

"I took the call and I had my notes in front of me. ...I wanted to tell her about all the great things we were doing—our programs and accomplishments. I had it all worked out in my head how it would go."

It never occurred to Troy that the reporter would have other ideas about the scope of the interview. She had done her own research and in the process discovered that one of Troy's clients had recently been investigated for a series of wrongdoings, one of which was embezzlement, and that their books had been audited.

"My client was being investigated, so of course, the books were audited. That is standard practice during an investigation. There was nothing inappropriate going on and my client was exonerated as expected," Troy explained.

Troy was quite sure he could explain the situation to the reporter and get the interview back on track, but she was persistent.

"I kept talking and she kept taking notes and I kept thinking I could pull myself out of the ditch by saying just one more thing. The next thing you know, I heard myself say, 'Yes, there was an investigation but we were cleared of all charges,'" he told me breathlessly.

"That's when I knew I had done myself in."

Troy was never able to recover the interview and things ended uncomfortably. The reporter wrote about his accomplishments and his nomination but the quote about being cleared of all charges also made it into the article.

"It didn't ruin our business or lose us any clients. It didn't even tarnish our reputation. But it did make me leery about talking to the press again."

Troy learned a good lesson about talking to journalists. They have a job to do and they have their own agenda. Sometimes that works in your favor, sometimes not. Most of the time a fluff piece is not going to turn into a piece of hard news, but you should be prepared for anything.

continued

The more prepared you are, the less likely you will be caught off guard, and that should give you a better chance of getting an article that really helps grow your Nexpertise!

Chapter 113. Getting and Giving Your Nexpert Print/ Radio Interview: Your Assignments for Days 67–80

Days 67–68: Start brainstorming about your angle. Think about your target audience and get three ideas for a story on paper (use the worksheet in Chapter 103).

Day 69: Do the research and pick out five media outlets you would like to target. Make sure you try both print and radio. And pick out media that speak directly to your target audience.

Day 70: Research the journalists in these media outlets. Who are they? What do they like to write/talk about? Will your story angle interest them and their readership? Know the journalists before you start working out your pitch.

Day 71: Craft the perfect pitch (as a phone pitch, pitch letter, or press release). Use the worksheets and directions in this section to make it as seamless as possible.

Days 72–75: Start pitching and/or sending out your press release. Follow up with phone calls. Schedule interviews. If you don't get the desired response, target five more local media outlets and keep trying.

Days 76–79: Prepare for your print and radio interviews and do them. Work the press!

Days 80: Follow up with your thank-you. Keep any and all articles for your media kit and website. Bask in the glow of your Nexpertise!

Record One Tele-Seminar

"You gotta have a gimmick if you want to get ahead."

—*Gypsy Rose Lee*

Chapter 114. Let's Push a Little Harder, Shall We?

You are now in the ascent of your Nexpertise, and I want you to keep going.

The momentum you create now will energize and ignite your business. It will keep the fire burning under you and will keep you growing, changing, and innovating.

By now, you should see some big changes with your business. It should feel different—more connected to the world and your customers. You should have a new purpose; one that is focused on meeting the demands of your niche audience with new products and services.

Whether you are a Lifestyle Guru or a Growth Maven, this will help you make your dream business a reality. You are on the way.

Now, I'm going to ask you to take a little trip into a world that might seem a bit foreign to you. But you've given speeches and written articles, so this should be a walk in the park for you!

I want you to put your toe in the water of Internet marketing. It will be good for you to see if you can use some tried and true Internet marketing tools to push your business forward a little more. So for this last big assignment in your first 100 days, I want you to put together one tele-seminar.

I know. I know. You're probably thinking, "Aren't tele-seminars for those long-winded, sales-y guys who sell e-books with titles like *10 Things Your Heart Surgeon Wished He Knew Before He Stepped into the Operating Room* and try to seduce you into buying that second set of Ginzu knives for just one payment of $19.99?

Well, maybe some of them are, but a tele-seminar is a respected form of Internet marketing. It's a great way for you to check in with your niche audience and for them to check in with you. It's a sales tool, but it's also a value-added service. And that's why I think it might make your business even stronger.

Read on. What have you got to lose?

Chapter 115. What Exactly Is a Tele-Seminar, and Why in Heaven's Name Do I Want to Host One?

A tele-seminar is a seminar or an interview you conduct over the phone.

Yes, I'm asking you to do something again that theoretically doesn't even require that you wear pants! Don't you just love that?

You arrange a time for the seminar and post an invitation on the web for everyone to see. You let your customers, colleagues, and e-mail list know all the specifics—date, time, and topic—beforehand: when the time comes, they call in to a specified phone number, then listen to you answering questions in an interview format and generally providing them with the knowledge of your Nexpertise.

You can also use the tele-seminar format to create an interactive exchange with small groups of your customers. You can open up the lines so they can ask you questions and freely exchange ideas with each other. Think of this as one big conference call where you can conduct weekly or monthly telephone coaching, consulting, and/or brainstorming sessions. The beauty is that you can create a tele-seminar that highlights your strengths as a Nexpert and provides an optimal experience for participants.

Think about it. You get to promote your products and services without having to conspicuously sell, and your niche audience gets to learn tips and tricks that will help them improve their lives and businesses. Or even better, maybe the tele-seminar becomes a new service that you provide to your customers—one that they are more than happy to pay for!

Tele-seminars are a low-fuss way to create a win-win for you and your customers.

And no one has to leave her house or get out of her pajamas to hear you speak. There are no traveling expenses or waste of time.

So, let's go through the details…

Chapter 116. Tele-Seminar Basics—The Technical Stuff

Some entrepreneurs resist doing tele-seminars because they think these might be complicated to set up.

Really, it's a breeze!

You just have to get familiar with the weird-sounding names of the tools used in the call setup. Most VAs are pretty skilled at setting up these tele-seminars, so ask your VA to do it for you. She's probably already a seasoned pro!

You'll need three basic components:

1. **A conference (or bridge) line.** This is a service that sets up and carries your tele-seminar. You can find good ones all over the Net. The service you pick should be able to handle upward of 200 to 300 people and should offer you the opportunity to record the content of the seminar. You can also use an operator who can direct the call-ins, and serve as a traffic cop of sorts (although this is usually not necessary).

   There are free lines and paid ones. You should weigh the costs versus the services you need. Yes, the paid ones offer more bells and whistles, but if you want to keep it simple, the free ones are just fine for your first tele-seminar.

2. **An automated registration system.** There are many services and/or tools to automate your registrations (do a Google search for tele-seminars). This means that your participants can sign up at either a dedicated online registration page or directly on your website. Either way, you will get a list of the people who signed up, with the date and time of their response. Many of these tools have a built in auto-responder system that will automatically send out notices at pre-determined times, to remind participants as the date of the seminar approaches and follow up with them after the tele-seminar.

   The follow-up is crucial here and this system will allow you to capture the names, e-mail addresses, and sometimes the phone numbers of participants. You will want to stay in touch with them; you can send them a transcript of the tele-seminar, a link to the recording, details about your products and services, and an invitation to your next tele-seminar.

   You should always have something else to offer them or invite them to—that's another reason to stay connected to them.

3. **A recording and transcription of your seminar.** You should always have the conference line service record your tele-seminar. If they can't do it, find a better service. This is pretty standard now. Remember, this seminar is now your intellectual property (make sure you get written sign-offs for this from the person you interviewed or who interviewed you), and you can then turn around and use it again as website content, a podcast, or a transcript to give to the participants as a follow-up gesture.

Chapter 117. Okay, I'm Game—What Do I Do First?

I'm pretty predictable.

You've been reading this book long enough now to know your first step.

As always, you must identify your niche audience and determine a tele-seminar subject that will attract and inform them. Your subject should be the solution to a common problem.

You must know them and what they need.

Sounds familiar, right?

If you're not sure (and at this point, you probably should be), use your tele-seminar to do a little market research. Here's what you can do:

■ Choose a topic that you know is of broad interest to your niche audience. By broad, I mean a subject that the majority of people in your niche are struggling to manage. This will attract more people on the call, and will help you develop a profile about everyone in your niche audience. That's what you want when you do market research.

The title of your tele-seminar might be *25 Strategies to Help Working Moms Balance Work and Family and Have More Quality Time for Both.* That will interest many working women, and you can use that as an opportunity to get to know them.

■ When people register for your seminar, ask them to fill out a questionnaire. This is your opportunity to ask them questions that will help you understand their problems and needs.

For instance, going with our working moms seminar, you might want to ask questions like: What are some of the biggest time-wasters in your day? What are the jobs/obligations you find you never have time to complete? What are some of the things you would like to do more often but never get the time?

These questions are designed to help you target problem areas that are the most important to your audience. You can also take the direct approach and ask, "If I could help you solve two problems today, what would they be?" This forces participants to write down what they hope to gain from listening to your seminar, and that will help you meet their needs.

Participants will send the completed questionnaire back to you after they register. You'll have time to read these and tailor your content to meet the needs of your audience.

Tele-seminars as an inexpensive market research tool—fantastic!

Chapter 118. Who Is My Niche Audience? What Do They Need to Know?

Let's say for the sake of argument that you don't need to do any research because you've been following along in this book, and after having done articles and talks, you know exactly who you are dealing with and what they are clamoring to know.

Let's get some ideas on paper.

List three problems facing your niche audience:

Problem #1:

_____

_____

_____

_____

Problem #2:

_____

_____

_____

_____

Problem #3:

_____

_____

_____

_____

Now, look over these problems and decide which one you are best capable of helping them manage. Consider how your products and services will correspond to this solution. The subject should make them want to know more.

After you have chosen the best area for your Nexpertise, let's work that idea into a tele-seminar title.

Your title should grab the audience's attention and be clear and specific about what people can expect to hear; for example: *Learn the Five Simple Things You Can Do Every Day to Save Your Ailing Marriage from Divorce.*

Now, you try it. Write down the title for your seminar topic and keep fiddling with it until you feel it really captures the essence of the talk.

_____

_____

_____

_____

Don't be afraid to ask trusted friends and colleagues what they think when they hear it. When you have the title and subject of your talk down, you can choose a format for your tele-seminar.

Chapter 119. The First Format—The Interview

The format is the style of your seminar. And there are many ways to skin this cat.

I'm going to list the options here and in the next chapter, but I'll give special attention to the first one because I think it is the best format for your first tele-seminar.

It requires no script, so it isn't as time-consuming as preparing a formal talk. Also, the act of being asked questions allows you to do a lively, engaging chat that is still custom built to your message.

Still, it's your talk, so I will go through all the options and you can do whatever best highlights your Nexpertise!

The Interview

This format allows you to craft a list of questions that support your message. Someone who will serve as a guide and host will interview you. The interviewer should be someone who knows you and your business, such as a trusted colleague or business partner.

This person can also be a strategic partner with a complementary business. For instance, if you are doing a seminar about *The 10 Things Every Entrepreneur Should Know Before They Start a Blog,* your interviewer might be an expert business blogger and small business consultant. In this scenario, his expertise might be helpful and impressive, and you could get a fee for every caller who becomes his client because of your seminar.

Whether you choose to do that or have a colleague interview you, be mindful that the interviewer should speak slowly and clearly. He should know your business; that way, if there are last-minute changes or points that need to be clarified during the talk, he can help lead you. He should not take away from your spotlight by talking too much, interjecting, or asking long-winded questions.

The interviewer's job is to be the conveyor belt. He must keep things moving, clarify anything confusing, dig for more details, keep it lively and interesting, and help you recover if you are nervous, faltering, or get off track. It's a big job, so don't choose someone you like to play pool with. Choose someone who can keep the conveyor belt moving.

The interviewer should introduce the tele-seminar and say a few words about your background and the things that make you a Nexpert. He should tell the audience what the guidelines are for the talk. For instance, you may want to open the lines at the end for a Q&A session. Whatever rules you decide on, the interviewer will be your rule keeper.

A word about preparation: Write out the questions ahead of time. Practice them and do several run-throughs with your interviewer. Remove anything that falls flat or is off message. Have the questions in front of you during the interview, with notes to help you remember the story that supports a certain point or an important idea you absolutely must get across.

Another variation on this format is that you can be the interviewer and interview another Nexpert.

You should interview someone with some cachet in your niche. For instance, you can interview a famous chef for your tele-seminar on *The Inside Secrets of Starting Your Own Catering Business,* or you can interview Miss South Carolina for your call about *The Ten Things You Have to Do to Help Your Teenager Win Beauty Pageants.*

This kind of format is often a treat for your listeners because they may not have previously heard this person speak or get grilled by you. In this type of tele-seminar you are often helping your guest promote their product or service, and presumably you're getting a piece of the action for endorsing it to your customer list. You could also team up with this person and develop a product/service together. The ways you can work together for profit are endless.

Whether you do the interviewing or get interviewed—or both—this is a team sport. If you both work well together, this might be an excellent first tele-seminar for you and your audience.

Chapter 120. The Other Two Formats—The Monologue and the Q&A

These next two formats are the most common after the interview.

Think about which one best suits your personality and will help you connect with your audience.

The Monologue

This is, simply, you talking to your customers and them listening.

If you are a dynamic speaker with lots to say and want to take the stage for an hour and wow them with your talk, this might be a great option for you.

Most newbies find this option a little daunting. For one thing, it's all about you and that means if you freak out in the middle of it, no one will be there to take some of the heat off you or help you get back on track. It also requires you to do some intense preparation; basically, you will have to write and pull off an hour-long speech. That is labor intensive.

Still, if you are a charismatic personality and think you will be able to really connect with your customers this way, consider it. But make sure you don't drone on and on about some cardboard subject. If you don't want people doing their e-mail while you're talking—or worse, hanging-up—it better be compelling, funny, and attention grabbing!

The Q&A

This format does not have a prepared talk. It is a great alternative for people who want to use the tele-seminar as a way to check in with their customers and be a present force in helping them solve their problems. It also helps if you are skilled at coming up with answers and good points off the top of your head.

This format is a bit like hosting a coaching session. You want a few people— maybe your best clients—and you let them grill you with questions and ideas. The advantage of the Q&A format is that interesting things happen here because the talk is not static or over-prepared, and clients really have time to air out their concerns or problems. This is a compelling format for really working through people's issues and challenges.

To work in this format, you should have a good rapport with your customers, and you should be sure that your audience has prepared questions, since they won't be reacting to a formal talk.

I suggest sending registrants e-mails before the seminar and asking them to come to the table with questions and comments about a specific topic. You should give them clear directions so they come up with questions that help the flow of the seminar. This will prevent long, embarrassing periods of silence.

The danger of this format is that doing only Q&A for an hour can be pretty grueling, especially if some of the questions catch you off guard or are confrontational. I think this format works well if you want to check in with a group of high-level clients and just chew the fat about some specific problems they are having, but all in all, this type of format is probably not the best choice for your first tele-seminar.

So, which format is right for you? Let's pick one and go with it:

a. The Interview, where you get interviewed
b. The Interview, where you do the interviewing
c. The Monologue
d. The Q&A

Chapter 121. Creating Your First Nexpert Tele-Seminar

Now you have all the information you need to start conducting your own tele-seminar. You know your audience, you know what they need, and you have a topic, title, and format. Now, it's time to start preparing your talk.

I'm going to help you create an interview format, where you're the one being interviewed. Here's how:

Step 1. Start with the title at the top of the page and start outlining ideas and concepts that support the topic.

Step 2. If you're drawing a blank, research your topic on the Internet and pull out ideas that will help get you writing.

Step 3. Write down some questions. Put yourself in your customers' place and think about what they want to know. You only have a short time to make an impression, so keep the questions smart, compelling, and super-important. Don't waste time on piddling little ideas. You want callers to walk away saying, "Wow, that woman really gave me some great ideas!"

Step 4. Go through your questions and start answering them. Do whatever research you need to do to come up with a thorough and comprehensive answer.

Step 5. Whittle down the answers so they are compact and efficient, but still carry the important information.

Step 6. Go over your questions and answers, and choose the best ones.

Step 7. Start working with your interviewer. Practice the interview. Take out questions that don't work. Add new things. Talk about what surprises there might be. Tell your interviewer about your weaker areas and where you may need help.

Step 8. Draft the interviewer's opening and closing comments and any rules for the call.

Step 9. Finalize the questions. Write them down and make a cheat sheet with notes on your answers.

Step 10. Do several beginning-to-end run-throughs as if the call were taking place.

Step 11. Be a Nexpert! Do your first tele-seminar!

To Charge or Not to Charge; That Is the Question

I suggest that your first tele-seminar be a freebie.

This will help you get your feet wet, and see how and if tele-seminars will play a role in your business. If you love it and can really bring the house down on your call, you can always create a series of tele-seminars (maybe the tele-seminar-of-the-month club) and develop a new stream of cash for your business.

If you want to use the tele-seminar as a way to get a closer connection to your customers and sell more of your products and services—which is what I suspect is more the case here—then I would go with the freebie.

Keep it simple. You want to focus on your core business so you can either grow like gangbusters or have more leisure time.

The freebie is a great way to establish yourself as an even bigger Nexpert, increase your mailing list, and keep you informed about your customer base and their changing needs. You also do not have the pressure that comes with a paid seminar; because it's free, people are more inclined to check it out. They may show you their gratitude by buying your other products and services. Once again, if you impress people with the great information they are getting for free, they have to wonder how much greater the paid information will be!

Whatever you do, make sure the tele-seminar supports your goals. Don't take your eye off the prize. That's how you get the business of your dreams!

Chapter 122. Tele-Seminars 101

Here's everything you need to know to make your tele-seminar an excellent forum for your Nexpertise!

- **Know your niche audience.** Know what they need. Yeah, yeah, you know my spiel!
- **Listen to a couple of tele-seminars in advance.** You may have heard them before, but listen to a couple with the intention of examining how they work, what you like or dislike about them, and how they are structured. This will give you some ideas for your own.
- **Know the length of your tele-seminar in advance.** Think about the topics you want to cover and the problem you want to help your audience solve. If you have 10 strategies to discuss, figure you'll spend roughly 5 to 6 minutes on each one. A 20-minute Q&A will put your tele-seminar at around 75 minutes. If you want to do a longer Q&A, cut down the number of points. Working it that way means your talk won't be rushed. Preparation is key!
- **Connect with participants before the seminar.** Send them a questionnaire and get to know their problems and challenges. Or send them reminders about the seminar. Either way, be a visible force in their lives until the seminar begins. It will keep them from getting distracted and forgetting about you.
- **Put a sign on the door that says "Teleconference In Progress!"** You really don't want your wife screaming at you about leaving your underwear in the kitchen while 30 or 40 customers listen in. Enough said.
- **Start on time.** Really, do I have to even say this?
- **Before the tele-seminar starts, do a roll call of the attendees on the call** (you can only do this with small groups). This way you know who is on the line with you. You may be surprised to find out who is there and not there. Be prepared to adjust your talk accordingly.
- **Do your welcome spiel.** Introduce yourself (or have your interviewer introduce you) and tell them why you are a Nexpert. Give them some background, but don't spend more than a minute or two on this. People don't want to hear about how

you pulled yourself up from a life of poverty on the mean streets of Cape Cod. They're here to have you change *their* lives!

- **Begin with a story that underscores your message.** Tell a short (one minute) story that underscores why you are hosting this seminar and what you want them to get out of it. The story will set up a personal feel and illuminate why you are all there.

- **Stick to lists and tips.** The "10 ways to..." and "25 strategies for..." can keep you on track moving from topic to topic. If you are being interviewed, have the questions laid out in front of you with notes of stories and facts you want to add. Have the interviewer give you cues if you are getting off message or are behind schedule.

- **Open the discussion for questions.** Most of the good stuff happens in the Q&A. It is an opportunity for callers to get a personal take on their unique challenges and a chance for you to shine as the Nexpert.

- **Conclude and go back over your points.** At the end of your seminar, you should go back over your points, reiterate your message, and mention the one specific product or service you want to sell during this tele-seminar. Trying to sell more than one thing at a time is usually ineffective. Your product or service should solve or be directly related to the problems or issues discussed in your tele-seminar. For instance, if you are helping executive assistants better utilize their time in the

Five Things You Can Do with Your Tele-Seminar Recording

1. Create a CD or downloadable MP3 that you can give to your customers as a free gift to entice sales.
2. Give a transcript of the tele-seminar to participants as a parting gift.
3. Set up a link on your website so customers can hear the talk in its entirety.
4. Set up the talk as a podcast that can be downloaded from iTunes to people's iPods.
5. Create a library of Nexpert information on your website that further defines you as the Nexpert in your field.

office, this might be a good opportunity to introduce them to your incredible desk organizer, but asking them to buy a new desk for their homes is going to fall flat.

- **Let people know you are looking for input.** Need some true stories for that e-book you're planning to write? (Wow! You are moving way ahead!) This is the time to let people know you would love to get their stories and use them in the book. Most people are happy to contribute their experiences. It makes them feel important.

- **Thank everyone and get off the phone.** Let them know how you'll be following up with them and do it. Be predictable.

Chapter 123. How to Get Your Audience to Listen to Your Tele-Seminar

About 50 percent of the people who say they are going to call in to a tele-seminar don't. There are many reasons for this, most of which seem to revolve around the distractions of everyday life. People intend to, but life gets in the way and they don't make it.

Five Things You Can Do to Follow Up

Whatever you do next should be accompanied by two words; "Thank you."

1. *Send them a transcript or CD of your seminar.*
2. *Invite them to your next public appearance, talk, or tele-seminar.*
3. *Direct them to your website, where they will get a discount for your products and services because they participated in the call.*
4. *Invite them to continue the phone discussion on your blog.*
5. *Send them a tip sheet/booklet with strategies that will expand on the tele-seminar and continue to help them improve their lives and/or business.*

Know this: Just because people don't call in doesn't mean they're not interested. You should still connect with them. Send them a link to a recording of the tele-seminar that they missed, invite them to your next one, tell them about your next speaking engagement, whatever, but view them as interested. Otherwise why would they have signed up in the first place, right?

There are some ways you can help drive people to your tele-seminar and get them to call in. There are no sure things, but these will help:

- Publicize your seminar on your website and newsletters.
- Put the topic, date, and time in your signature on your e-mails.
- Send an e-mail to everyone on your mailing list.
- Send out postcards with a personal message to good customers you know might have a special interest.
- Use the auto-responder feature to remind people about the upcoming talk: a few weeks before, a week before, a couple of days before, and on the morning of your talk.
- Give registrants quizzes, e-mails, or homework to complete before the talk. It piques their interest and creates a greater investment in calling in.
- Have your announcement on the website and in the newsletters of your strategic partners and have them e-mail your invitation to their list.
- Post the details of the tele-seminar in places where your audience hangs out online: favorite blogs, chat rooms, etc.
- About bloggers, see if you can get a few of them to cover the tele-seminar or interview you before or after the talk.

Chapter 124. Putting Your Nexpert Tele-Seminar to Work for You: Your Assignments for Days 81–99

It's time to plan and execute your first tele-seminar:

Day 81: Decide what problems and challenges are facing your niche audience and lay out three problems in the exercise in Chapter 118. Pick one issue that highlights your Nexpertise and compose a title. Keep working the title until it is compelling and attention getting.

Day 82: Fiddle with your topic and title until it is smooth. Choose a format: one of the two interview formats, a monologue, or Q&A. Schedule a date and time for your tele-seminar. Research conference line companies and their features. Choose one, contact them, and set a date and time for your tele-seminar.

Days 83–85: Start promoting your tele-seminar. Choose several strategies from Chapter 123. (This will be ongoing. Do a bit every day.) And get out there and start promoting your talk. As people register, make contact with them and have the auto-responder system send them updates and e-mails. You may want to send them a questionnaire as they register. Prepare that now.

Days 86–93: Work the steps in Chapter 121 to create and hone your program. Keep in mind that you must practice. If you are using an interviewer, you must schedule time to rehearse together.

Day 94: Keep honing and promoting your talk up to the day of your tele-seminar, and devise a follow-up strategy using the ideas in the sidebar to Chapter 123.

Day 95: Give the tele-seminar—revel in your Nexpertise!

Days 96–98: Put your follow-up plan into gear. Say "thanks," send a free gift, give a discount, and follow up with new information. Be sure you use this opportunity to make a connection!

Day 99: Feel great that you tried something new and risky. Feel good that people took time out of their busy day to hear what you had to say! You are truly a maverick and a Nexpert! Well-done!

Nexpert Story: Jonathan Miller

 Jonathan Miller was not in the information products business.

He began with a small antique store he started in his backyard pool house in Long Island. His exquisite taste and eye for unique and beautiful pieces, as well as his ability to sniff out bargains at garage and estate sales, quickly helped his business grow.

Soon, he was out of the pool house and into a cozy, well-located retail space in Chelsea, the renowned antiques district in New York City. Jonathan was excited about playing with the big boys in Manhattan, but his store was small and he needed a way to attract the attention of collectors and bigger buyers.

"I looked around me and I was surrounded by huge players. It was impossible to set myself apart from the crowd. I needed a way to speak directly to people who specialized in collecting antiques in my niche, and I needed to connect with the big buyers—not just the special-occasion buyer."

Jonathan and I discussed several options, but he was intrigued with the tele-seminar idea. Even I thought it was a bit of a stretch—selling antiques in a tele-seminar—but Jonathan proved my adage that entrepreneurs know their business better than anyone else. He knew instinctively about his strengths and he knew he could reach his core audience of buyers this way.

"I knew the big buyers well and I knew what challenges they faced. I knew they were passionate and avid about collecting, but I also knew they weren't professionals and they made mistakes—often costly ones."

Jonathan set up his first tele-seminar. He called it The Ten Ways that Estate Sales are Ripping Off Antique Collectors. He sent it out to his customer list and the big buyers. He put it on his website, posted signs at popular flea markets in the area, and talked about it in some key collector chat rooms.

"I got 82 people signed up for my first talk and 53 actually called in. I gave them ten things that I thought were happening right under their noses and ways to handle the problems head-on when they were buying. I gave them valuable tips that I knew most of them did not know, and I gave them real advice on how to defend themselves and save a lot of money."

continued

The talk sent the message that Jonathan was knowledgeable and honest. It positioned him as a Nexpert and an advocate.

"The Q&A also worked well because I had time to answer their personal collecting problems and I really was able to show my expertise and send the message that I could be trusted.

This was not the last tele-seminar Jonathan did.

"I do one or two a month on different topics. Always free. I have a lot of return traffic, but those people are also buying from me consistently, so I welcome having a closer relationship with them."

Jonathan's tele-seminars have helped him get a national customer base and he has orders from private buyers all over the country.

"The tele-seminar really helped me stay local but take my business nationally. It positioned me as one of the big boys before I was one of them."

Now, of course, he is one of them!

The Wrap Up: Days 67–99

WRAP-UP

Write a Press Release and Set Up Two Media Interviews

Days 67–68: Start brainstorming about your angle. Think about your target audience and get three ideas for a story on paper (use the worksheet in Chapter 103).

Day 69: Do the research and target five media outlets. Make sure you try both print and radio. And pick out media that speak directly to your target audience.

Day 70: Do research on the journalists in these media outlets. Who are they? What do they like to write/talk about? Will your story angle interest them and their readership? Know the journalists before you start working out your pitch.

Day 71: Craft the perfect pitch (as a phone pitch, pitch letter, or press release). Use the worksheets and directions in this section to make it as seamless as possible.

Days 72–75: Start pitching and/or sending out your press release. Follow up with phone calls. Schedule interviews. If you don't get the desired response, target five more local media outlets. Keep trying.

Days 76–79: Prepare for your print and radio interviews and do them. Work the press!

Days 80: Follow up with thank-you calls. Keep any and all articles for your media kit and website.

Prepare and Give a Tele-Seminar

Day 81: Decide what problems and challenges are facing your niche audience and lay out three problems in the exercise in Chapter 118. Pick one issue that highlights your Nexpertise and compose a title. Keep working the title until it is compelling and attention getting.

Day 82: Fiddle with your topic and title until they are smooth. Choose a format: one of the two interview formats, a monologue, or Q&A. Schedule a date and time for your tele-seminar. Research conference line companies and their features. Choose one, contact them, and set a date and time for your tele-seminar.

Days 83–85: Promote your tele-seminar. Choose several strategies from Chapter 123. (This will be ongoing. Do a bit every day.) Get out there and start promoting your talk. As people register, contact them and have the auto-responder system send them updates and e-mails. You may want to send them a questionnaire as they register. Prepare that now.

Days 86–93: Work the steps in Chapter 121 to create and hone your program. Keep in mind that you must practice. If you are using an interviewer, you must schedule time to rehearse together.

Day 94: Keep honing and promoting your talk up until the day of your tele-seminar, and set up a follow-up strategy using the follow-up ideas in the sidebar in Chapter 123.

Day 95: Give the tele-seminar—revel in your Nexpertise!

Days 96–98: Put your follow-up plan into gear. Say "thanks," send a free gift, give a discount, and follow up with new information. Use this opportunity to make a connection.

Day 99: Feel great that you tried something new and risky. Feel good that people took time out of their busy day to hear what you had to say. You are truly a maverick and a Nexpert! Well done!

Part

From Your "Home Office From Hell" to a Thriving, Growing, Innovating Success in 100 Days

"Seventy percent of success in life is showing up."

—Woody Allen

Chapter 125. Your New Life as a Nexpert!

What you have now is momentum.

Here is what has hopefully transpired for you:

You started reading this in your pajamas in your home office cave. Back then, your business was in a rut. Things were moving along slowly and you had some success, but somewhere along the way things started to stand still. You hoped this book would spark something in you because you were looking for a little inspiration, a way to make things work again.

But you never needed inspiration—you needed action! You needed to do something every day to help pull your business out of the rut.

So even if you didn't follow this book to the letter—even if you decided to write one more article and forgo the public speaking, or you loved the Tips Booklet idea but thought the whole tele-seminar thing wasn't your bag, or you got a VA but decided to wait on the virtual office—I still hope you did one thing every day.

Because if you did, your business is better today than it was three months ago.

There is no substitute for getting up every morning and doing one small task that will help you change your business. And now that you are a Nexpert (you know you deserve the title) and you have some successes under your belt, you can't possibly stop now. You have to keep doing a little bit every day to further your Nexpertise, take some risks and get out there in front of your niche audience.

Inertia breeds more inertia. Momentum inspires more momentum.

You are surfing on a big wave right now and you have to stay on the board.

Keep going. Good things will happen.

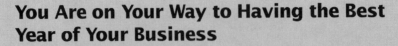

You Are on Your Way to Having the Best Year of Your Business

This is what I hope you learned in the past three months:

- *You can have the business of your dreams.*
- *You are tough enough to take risks to make your business even stronger.*
- *You can do things that scare the hell out of you.*
- *You can embrace change and see it as an opportunity.*
- *You are truly an entrepreneur, a maverick.*
- *You know there is no stopping you now because you have momentum.*
- *You have only just started to see what you are capable of doing!*

Chapter 126. One Nexpert Puts It All Together!

Manny Montega had the dream in the cubicle, just like you.

Manny worked for a New York communications company that served the private equity industry. When he made senior vice president, he should've been overjoyed. Instead, he was extremely unhappy.

"The atmosphere was vile. The personalities were ugly, too much screaming and back-biting, and to boot, I was working in a communications company where people couldn't communicate," he told me.

"I knew I could do better."

And that's all it takes for the dream in the cubicle to take hold. You know in your heart of hearts that you can do a better job. And that's what you set out to do.

So that's what Manny did.

One day he gave notice and set up shop in his second bedroom in his Manhattan apartment.

"And that's kind of where I stayed," he confessed. "I had clients. I was making enough money. I liked being my own boss and working on my own, but I never really got much further.

"I guess I was tired of the rat race, and after I left the firm, I hunkered down, laid low, and licked my wounds. That was fine for a while, but then it started being the way I ran my business. One day, I looked around me and thought, 'Is this really all my business can be?'"

That was the moment Manny realized the extended vacation was over and he needed to do something new every day. We sketched out a plan to move him forward in small daily steps—one small, underwhelming task every day.

This process set him up for success. It didn't require that he turn his life upside down and climb a mountain every day. It required a slight shift in his work habits on a consistent basis.

"I thought of it like grass growing; if you watch grass grow every day, it doesn't seem like much is happening. But if you look at your lawn after two weeks, you see that it has grown a lot," he explained.

I think Manny's metaphor is exactly what this book is about; it is the formula for success in moving your business to new heights. And that's exactly what happened for Manny.

Manny did most of his work at home, but he met new and existing clients in the conference rooms he rented in a downtown executive suite. He hired a VA (who also acted as his bookkeeper) and a freelance accountant.

"Because I got some help with the administrative stuff, I spent more time doing the revenue-producing things that I did as a senior vice president. It made me feel like a boss again," he told me.

"The change was more psychological than it was about the jobs I was handing off. My head changed. I had more space in my head to take on the role of CEO. And when that happened, it jumpstarted the rest, and everything moved forward from there at a crazy pace."

Manny jumped on the wave of momentum and rode it.

Within six months, he moved out of his bedroom office and opened a small boutique firm in the Financial District.

"We found a shared space that was a huge loft. It was relaxed, kind of hip, and very low-key," he said.

"The space was informal enough that it defined us as being different from the buttoned-up competition. We were the young, cool upstarts who still had a lot of agency experience behind us."

The move set the tone for Manny's company. He brought on a talented partner, hired young exuberant staff, and defined a vision for his company.

"We could deliver great communications programs for the private equity market, but we could do it better and be more innovative than the stodgy firms who were set in their ways," he told me.

"We could tap into that experience, but put a healthy new spin on it."

With his staff in place, Manny set out to conquer the next frontier.

He became a Nexpert.

He gave talks at industry conferences and hosted a panel for some of the biggest players in the industry. He wrote a monthly column in the leading industry magazine, giving private equity companies ideas about how to improve their communications with their portfolio companies.

He wrote a series of Tips Booklets that he uses in his media kit and on his website to help potential customers get a sense of what he can do for them.

"It is crucial for my business that I am out there talking to my audience. I have to be a present and formidable opinion-maker. My name and the company's name have to be in the public space and constantly mentioned or I'll lose business," Manny said.

"People will forget that I can make a difference to their business, so I have to remind them constantly."

And he doesn't do that by reading his résumé. He does it by giving away information and showing that this is just the tip of the iceberg.

Manny's company took over most of the shared office space they had been renting. He has six fulltime employees and four freelancers. He hit $2 million in revenue last year and expects that to continue. His company is considered to be one of the most innovative small firms in the industry.

"I knew I could have a successful business, but the walls of my bedroom office were like a barrier keeping me confined in a small space," he told me.

"I needed a jumpstart just to remind myself of what I was capable of creating."

Chapter 127. Basking in the Glow of Your Nexpertise: Your Assignment for Day 100

Day 100: Take a well-deserved break and feel great about the fact that your business is better and stronger and healthier than it was 99 days ago. You've only just started. This is the beginning of more great things to come.

Congratulations, you are a maverick entrepreneur!

Chapter 128. Taking Your Nexpert Status to the Next Level: The Second 100 Days

Yes, I plan to write another book of tasks that will help get you through the second 100 days, but until then, I want you to keep going.

Do more speeches. Write more articles. Try more tele-seminars. When something doesn't work, fix it and try it again. Keep trying until it works.

Not only will your business grow, you will also get stronger and more confident. You will be used to change. You will embrace new opportunities as an organic characteristic of your personality. That feeling will translate into your business. Customers and clients will sense it even if they can't name it. Your work will change; it will be more dynamic and creative.

You will start opening doors that get you closer to what you want: more money, more time, more satisfaction, and a better life. Work a little on that goal every day and eventually you'll get there. I am as sure of it as I am sure grass grows a little each day.

Now I want to hear from you. I want you to tell me your experiences: successes, failures, challenges, and triumphs. Write me at Landers@HomeOfficeSuccess.com.

I have to do my own market research—I need to know what worked or didn't work and why. I want to use your personal stories in the book for the second 100 days. I want to know what challenges you are facing now, and what you want to achieve.

That way, I can make sure the information I write about in the next book is the advice that will best help you have the business and the life of your dreams.

I look forward to hearing from you. Until then, do one small thing *today*!

Part

Appendix

The 100-Day Plan

The 100-Day Plan at a Glance

Day 1

All Aboard!

(Chapter 10) Be clear that you have a Home Office From Hell and are ready to change your business. Then, take the Quiz and discover who you are—a Lifestyle Guru or a Growth Maven.

Day 2

Lifestyle Gurus!		Growth Mavens!
Method 1: *(Chapter 45) Look through the Yellow Pages, do an online search, scan the classified real estate sections of your local newspapers, and scroll through the listings on Craigslist.*	**Method 2:** *(Chapter 45) Go to GetAVirtualOffice.com and get a virtual office!*	*(Chapter 29) Figure out how to find all of the available executive suites and shared office space located in your geographic area of interest.*

Day 3

(Chapter 45) Once you've completed your search and narrowed your list of executive suites in your preferred locations, start calling them to find out what virtual office space packages they offer and ask about prices.	*Everything for Days 3 to 7 was taken care of on Day 2, so you can make more money, develop something new for your business, get to the beach, or just kick back with a glass of wine and enjoy a little extra free time!*	*(Chapter 29) Once you've completed your search and narrowed your list of executive suites and/or shared office spaces in your preferred locations, start calling them to find out what spaces are available, costs, and more.*

Day 4

(Chapter 45) Narrow your list to no more than your five top choices and make an appointment to tour each location		*(Chapter 29) Narrow your list to no more than five top choices and make an appointment to tour each location.*

continued

Day 5	**Lifestyle Gurus!**		**Growth Mavens!**
	Method 1: *(Chapter 45) You should be able to visit all five locations in one day.*	**Method 2:** *Enjoy a little extra free time!*	*(Chapter 29) You should be able to visit all five locations in one day. Conduct the same type of due diligence that you would use if you were looking to rent an apartment. Go back to the checklists and make a list of questions to ask, things to look for, etc. Decide what is important to you and do not deviate from your plan.*
Day 6	*(Chapter 45) Sign the agreement and pay any up-front fees (security deposit, etc.).*		*(Chapter 29) Sign the agreement and pay any up-front fees (security deposit, etc.). Plan to make the move.*
Day 7	*Start using your new VO!*		*(Chapter 31) Contact the U.S. Postal Service and make a business address change. Get boxes. Make sure all the office paperwork is in order.*
Day 8	**Lifestyle Gurus!**		**Growth Mavens!**
	(Chapter 53) Make a general, sketchy list of which time-sucking jobs you want to delegate, and how many hours you currently devote to these chores.		*(Chapter 31) Decide how you will conduct the move. Make arrangements with people who will help you move and decide how you will repay them.*
Day 9	*(Chapter 56) Find yourself a good virtual staffing agency on the Internet.*		*(Chapter 31) Pack nonessential business items. Mark each box with a clear description and make a list of supplies you will need for the new office.*

Day 10	**Lifestyle Gurus!**	**Growth Mavens!**
	(Chapter 56) Contact the virtual staffing agency and discuss your specific needs and goals.	*(Chapter 31) Send out an announcement of your move. Get together all*
Day 11	*(Chapter 56) Finalize paperwork with the agency. Phone your new VA and say, "Hi!"*	*(Chapter 31) Shop for new supplies. pack more items. Check with office manager to confirm move-in time and*
Day 12	*(Chapter 56) Create a list of time-sucking jobs you will give to your VA with specific instructions, and your time expectations for each task. Send it to your new VA and follow up with a phone call. Set up a work schedule with your new VA.*	*(Chapter 31) Do the last business that needs to be done. Pack all the essential business items into a "Top Priority" box. Call helpers and have them meet at a single place at a specific time and let them know the plan. Get a handful of petty cash for tips.*
Day 13	*(Chapter 56) Get on to more important revenue-generating work.*	*(Chapter 31) Moving Day! Give everyone a task and set them to work. Set up the staging area while boxes are being moved in.*
Day 14	*(Chapter 57) Create your own organizational chart. Use the chart on page 87 to help you organize your decisions.*	*(Chapter 37) Make a list of which time-sucking jobs you want to delegate and how many hours you currently devote to these chores. Use the chart on page 57 to help you organize your decisions.*
Day 15	*(Chapter 57) Create a checklist for each of the jobs you want to outsource.*	*(Chapter 37) Find yourself a good virtual staffing agency.*
Day 16	*Continue creating your checklist.*	*(Chapter 37) Contact the virtual staffing agency and ask to speak with a project manager to discuss your specific needs and goals.*

All Lifestyle Gurus and Growth Mavens!

It's time to become a Nexpert!

continued

Day 17	**All Together Now!**
	Become a Nexpert
	Answer the question, "What does your business do?" in Chapter 62.

Day 18	*Start talking like a Nexpert. When people ask you about your business, tell them what you've written above and repeat it until it feels natural.*

Day 19	**Write Your Article and Get It Out to Publications**
	Define your niche audience. Complete the worksheet in Chapter 69. Buy some books about writing articles for magazines and newspapers.

Day 20	*Research where these customers are getting their information from and complete the worksheet in Chapter 70.*

Day 21	*Research these publications. Find out what kind of stories are being written and are of interest to your audience.*

Day 22	*Read about writing.*

Day 23	*Brainstorm ideas for stories, start an idea file, and add ideas as you go along.*

Day 24	*Create a pitch for the article and begin to call editors.*

Day 25	*Continue working on your pitch and calling editors.*

Day 26	*Continue...*

Day 27	*Call more editors and refine the pitch.*

Day 28	*Keep calling until someone likes your idea and wants to work with you.*

Day 29	*Create a one-page proposal of your article based on your conversation with the editor.*

Day 30	*Continue creating a one-page proposal of your article based on your conversation with the editor.*

Day 31	*Refine your proposal and send it to editor.*

Day 32	*Begin writing (or start looking for a ghostwriter). Call back editor(s).*

Day 33	**All Together Now!**
	Continue writing (or looking for a ghostwriter). Call back editor(s).
Day 34	*Continue...*
Day 35	
Day 36	
Day 37	
Day 38	
Day 39	*Ask for feedback. Take criticism. Make edits.*
Day 40	*Continue asking for feedback and making edits.*
Day 41	*Submit to editor.*
Day 42	**Prepare Your Talk and Set Dates**
	Fill in the blanks in Chapters 82, 83, and 84. Decide who is your audience, what message you want to send, and what kind of speech you will prepare.
Day 43	*Research the best speaking opportunities in your area. Look for organizations that are rich in your niche target audience and qualify as great speaking opportunities (use the criteria in Chapter 80). Contact and call the organizers.*
Day 44	*Continue researching the best speaking opportunities in your area. Look for organizations that are rich in your niche target audience and qualify as great speaking opportunities (use the criteria in Chapter 80). Continue making contact and calling organizers.*
Day 45	*Outline your talk and create a short, one-page proposal outlining what you will speak about, how long the talk will be, and the format in which you will deliver the talk (workshop, seminar, formal speech, etc.)*
Day 46	*Gather the materials to send to the organizers. This will include a short bio for them to send to attendees, a picture, and any other material that you feel helps position you as a Nexpert.*

continued

Day 47	**All Together Now!**
	Send out the proposal and information about you and your business by e-mail. Follow up with organizers after they receive your information. Call new ones and send them proposals. Be persistent; don't give up.
Day 48	*Continue...*
Day 49	
Day 50	*Write and prepare for your talk. Keep talking to new and existing organizers. Set dates for talks and firm up details.*
Day 51	*Continue writing and preparing for your talk. Keep talking to new and existing organizers. Set dates for talks and firm up details.*
Day 52	*Continue...*
Day 53	
Day 54	
Day 55	
Day 56	
Day 57	*Practice the talk in front of a mirror or camera. Critique yourself. Then give it to a practice audience or friend. Get feedback. Practice and work out the kinks.*
Day 58	*Rewrite and hone the speech. Practice giving the speech again to work out any final kinks, and have your practice audience throw questions at you for the Q&A session.*
Day 59	*Continue rewriting, honing, and practicing the speech. Finalize speaking dates and go over last minute issues.*
Day 60	*Continue...*

Day 61	**All Together Now!**
	Keep going over the speech every few days until you speak. When the time comes, enjoy that you finally got what you deserve—you are a Nexpert Speaker!

Day 62	**Write Your Tips Booklet**
	Remind yourself about your audience. Go to Chapter 92 and do the worksheet. Then pick the title for your booklet. There is an exercise in Chapter 92 to help you do that. If you go to Chapter 93, you will find some brainstorming strategies. Do the research and start brainstorming your tips. When you're done and your brain is fried, take a well-deserved break.

Day 63	*Take a look at your brainstorming and start to organize your tips. Look at Chapter 94 for guidance. There are specific directions there to help you get through it. Get a good substantial rough draft.*

Day 64	*Ask for feedback from trusted advisors. Finalize your draft. Lay out the text, contact info, and company logo. (You might need more time if you are using an outside designer.)*

Day 65	*Check the details, put the final product on a CD, and take it to a copy shop. Have them print out copies and bind them. Or print them and bind them yourself.*

Day 66	*In Chapter 98, I give you a bunch of different uses for the Tips Booklet. Finalize your strategy for how your Tips Booklet will help you, and fill in the exercise in that chapter. Keep going! Look what you are accomplishing!*

Day 67	**Write a Press Release and Set Up Two Media Interviews**
	Start brainstorming about your angle. Think about your target audience and get three ideas for a story on paper (use the worksheet in Chapter 103).

Day 68	*Continue brainstorming about your angle.*

Day 69	*Do the research and target five media outlets. Make sure you try both print and radio. And pick out media that speak directly to your target audience.*

Day 70	*Do research on the journalists in these media outlets. Who are they? What do they like to write/talk about? Will your story angle interest them and their readership? Know the journalists before you start working out your pitch.*

continued

Day 71	**All Together Now!**
	Craft the perfect pitch (as a phone pitch, pitch letter, or press release). Use the worksheets and directions in Part 7 to make it as seamless as possible.
Day 72	*Start pitching and/or sending out your press release. Follow up with phone calls. Schedule interviews. If you don't get the desired response, target five more local media outlets. Keep trying.*
Day 73	*Continue...*
Day 74	
Day 75	
Day 76	*Prepare for your print and radio interviews and do them. Work the press!*
Day 77	*Continue...*
Day 78	
Day 79	
Day 80	*Follow up with thank-you calls. Keep any and all articles for your media kit and website.*
Day 81	**Prepare and Give a Tele-Seminar**
	Decide what problems and challenges are facing your niche audience and lay out three problems in the exercise in Chapter 118. Pick one issue that highlights your Nexpertise and compose a title. Keep working the title until it is compelling and attention getting.
Day 82	*Fiddle with your topic and title until they are smooth. Choose a format: one of the two interview formats, a monologue, or Q&A. Schedule a date and time for your tele-seminar. Research conference line companies and their features. Choose one, contact them, and set a date and time for your tele-seminar.*
Day 83	*Promote your tele-seminar. Choose several strategies from Chapter 123. (This will be ongoing. Do a bit every day.) Get out there and start promoting your talk. As people register, contact them and have the auto-responder system send them updates and e-mails.*

Day 84	**All Together Now!**
	Continue promoting your tele-seminar. Use more of the strategies from Chapter 123. As people register, you may want to send them a questionnaire. Prepare that now.
Day 85	*Continue...*
Day 86	*Work the steps in Chapter 121 to create and hone your program. Keep in mind that you must practice. If you are using an interviewer, you must schedule time to rehearse together.*
Day 87	*Continue...*
Day 88	
Day 89	
Day 90	
Day 91	
Day 92	
Day 93	
Day 94	*Keep honing and promoting your talk up until the day of your tele-seminar, and set up a follow-up strategy using the follow-up ideas in the sidebar on page 201.*
Day 95	*Give the tele-seminar—revel in your Nexpertise!*
Day 96	*Put your follow-up plan into gear. Say "thanks," send a free gift, give a discount, and follow up with new information.*
Day 97	*Continue putting your follow-up plan into gear. Use this opportunity to make a connection.*
Day 98	*Continue...*

continued

Day 99	**All Together Now!**
	Feel great that you tried something new and risky. Feel good that people took time out of their busy day to hear what you had to say. You are truly a maverick and a Nexpert. Well done!

Day 100	Take a well-deserved break and feel great about the fact that your business is better and stronger and healthier than it was 99 days ago. You've only just started. This is the beginning of more great things to come.

Congratulations,
you are a maverick Nexpert entrepreneur!

INDEX

Dear Reader,

I wanted to thank you for buying and reading this book, by giving you a couple of special gifts that you can immediately use to improve your business. Here they are:

Special Gift Number One

The first gift is my completely free **Home Office Success Toolkit.** Now that you are inspired and energized to keep improving and growing your business, these new tools—which I will update frequently on my website, **www.HomeOfficeSuccessToolkit.com**—are my gift to you. The information and resources I lay out there will help you build on your success long after you've finished reading this book, and will help you take advantage of the momentum you've already created.

This is a terrific way for you to keep on building your business. I hope you'll come to **www.HomeOfficeSuccessToolkit.com** and see some of the great things we have put together for you.

Special Gift Number Two

The second gift is my personal favorite, because it involves learning from other entrepreneurs. I've put together a free CD that is chock-full of advice, stories of success and failure, and little gems of wisdom from some of our Nexpert entrepreneurs who have taken their businesses to the next level and lived to tell the tale. These Nexperts are part of our **Home Office Success Leaders Network** and they can tell you how to get where you want to go.

These Nexperts will give you candid, hard-won advice about the perils and pitfalls of creating and maintaining a thriving business. They'll help you become a recognized Nexpert by sharing their real experiences and inspiring you to make better choices for building your business.

There is no better way to learn than from those who have already achieved success, so join us at **www.HomeOfficeSuccessToolkit.com** to hear it right from the source.

Again, I want to thank you for reading my book and sharing my passion for entrepreneurship. I hope it was contagious and I hope you will continue along with us on this ride to make your homebased business a runaway success.

Best Regards,

Jeff Landers

Here are the businesses I'm involved with.
These businesses can help you make your homebased
business more productive and successful.

———————————

To Hire A Virtual Assistant
check out:
www.GetAVirtualAssistant.com/book

To Rent A Virtual Office Space
take a look at:
www.GetAVirtualOffice.com/book

To Find An Executive Suite or Shared Office Space
go to:
www.Offices2Share.com/book

For The Home Office From Hell® Merchandise
Visit our store at:
www.cafepress.com/officefromhell

Want More?

**Schedule A 30 Minute
Home Office Success™ Coaching Session
One-on-One With The Author**

After reading T*he Home Office From Hell Cure* you may find you are ready to take action, but you still have a few questions that are specific to your home-based business or your particular situation.

Well don't worry—you don't have to go it alone.

Jeff Landers will personally work with you, one-on-one, to get you going in the right direction.

Go to **www.TheHomeOfficeSuccessCoach.com/book** to schedule your appointment and start working towards a better business today.